I AM

I Am With You

WITH

DIVINE HELP FOR TODAY'S NEEDS

YOU

John Woolley

OLIVER
NELSON™

THOMAS NELSON PUBLISHERS
Nashville

Published in Nashville, Tennessee, by Thomas Nelson, Inc. U.S. edition licensed from Arthur James Ltd., 70 Cross Oak Road, Berkhamsted, Hertfordshire, HP4 3HZ, UK.

First published in Great Britain in 1984 by Crown (Great Britain).

The Bible version used in this publication is THE NEW KING JAMES VERSION. Copyright © 1979, 1980, 1982, Thomas Nelson, Inc., Publishers.

Library of Congress Cataloging-in-Publication Data

Woolley, John (John A.)
   I am with you : divine help for today's needs / John Woolley.
   p. cm.
   ISBN 0-7852-6973-8 (HC)
   1. Private revelations. 2. Spiritual life—Christianity. I. Title
BV5091.R4W66 1999
248.2'9—dc21
                                              99-23359
                                                  CIP

Printed in the United States of America.
1 2 3 4 5 6 — 04 03 02 01 00 99

Preface

I am with you always, even to the end of the age.
(Matt. 28:20)

From all over the world come messages of appreciation about these words of divine encouragement and guidance from the risen Lord Jesus Christ through His Holy Spirit, words received in prayer times by Father John Woolley, former British hospital chaplain. With the words came a promise by our Lord that there would be a wonderful spread of His Word—a promise now being marvelously realized.

I Am with You offers unique help for the often difficult Christian road, and it is an essential companion for times of prayer and Bible study. These words unfailingly bring a sense of God's nearness; they bring tranquillity, and they wonderfully strengthen. Church leaders and many readers of all Christian denominations speak constantly of being uplifted and inspired by this little book, often in a life-changing way.

Using This Book

Although the words in *I Am with You* are usually read in the order given in the book, there is an index for specific areas of personal need or sudden crises.

If prayer is made beforehand, many readers have found that they turn to just the right page and that a word for the need of the moment is unfailingly given.

The Bible Quotations

Bible verses—in which God speaks directly—have been chosen to accompany our Lord's words in *I Am with You.*

My Prayer for You

May the Lord Jesus Christ speak to your heart repeatedly through His words in this book.

May He greatly bless you, and each day draw you closer to Him.

I Am the Hope

I am the hope of all the ends of the earth. But so few truly know it deep in their hearts. In Me lies the fulfillment of the complex desires and possibilities of human nature.

You know that all the qualities you see in Me are available for you. Are you sad, My child, that so often you fail to make use of them? Yes, this is the world's failing—that men do not appropriate what is there for them in Me.

Set Me before you always as your one true hope. Be sure that your hand is firmly in Mine. Proclaim Me as mankind's hope to those around you. As you recognize the progress you make with Me, so the conviction will grow that you bring to telling others all that I can be to them!

I know that in your heart is the longing to know Me more perfectly. I honor that longing, and that is why you are sure of My patience in all your failures. It is, of course, My grace that helps you to maintain the longing and to come increasingly into oneness with Me.

The one who comes to Me I will by no means cast out.
(John 6:37)

Long Before My Love Was Seen

Long before My love was seen on earth, it was expressed in creativity. Although seen as creativity of power or of mystery, it is a creativity of love, a continuing creativity.

Existence, as you see it, is puzzling and often frightening, but let it thrill you that the Father was seen in His creation, becoming one with it, surrendering Himself to it. The moment in history when I stood as the meeting place of divine love and human hopes and fears was the beginning of all true spiritual awareness.

You will be aware of much darkness and of forces dedicated to obstructing your climb toward the heavenly sphere. Any other view of My creation would be naive and partial. Nevertheless, you must resolutely see love as the soul of creation—now, as it always was.

Love in creativity means that I am never remote from the inevitable heartaches of My children or, of course, from your heartaches.

He who has seen Me has seen the Father.
(John 14:9)

Dwell upon My Sacrifice

My child, let it be your privilege each day to dwell upon My sacrifice made for the whole world.

In My suffering love upon the cross you see a continuing process, the unrequited love that pursues My children—yearning for the slightest response and profoundly grateful when one of the children surrenders his life to Me.

On the cross, you see My heart of love crushed, for the moment, by the force of evil that darkens this universe. Then you see the bursting forth again of love's power in My Father's victory; this power, in its submission and its patience, can change permanently any human situation.

Although you are conscious of being unworthy of that love, be sure that the pain of rejection is made much less by even the simplest, imperfect dependence upon Me.

Here, at the cross, give Me your heart anew every day.

I lay down My life for the sheep.
(John 10:15)

3

Live Close to Me

*H*ow much it means to Me when one of My children, responding to a prompting of My Spirit, asks to live close to Me.

The response to that request is automatic. Forces to draw closer our spirits are then at work despite the tangled emotions and contrainfluences of earth. As soon as that hesitant request is made, I am able to look upon My child as perfected.

Everything is built upon that child's request. I see beyond the intermittent progress, the spiritual weariness, and the times when the child fails Me. I need no more than the initial response, and the continuance of that wish to be close to Me, for My existence increasingly to interpenetrate yours.

My child, can you still recognize the deep desire for closeness to Me in your heart, even after many discouragements in your spiritual walk? If so, let it remind you of the perfection that is your destiny.

I drew them with . . . bands of love.
(Hos. 11:4)

The Unbreakable Bond

My child, the bond between us is unbreakable because you are My chosen.

The company you keep is with the Architect of this universe in His infinite wisdom. My presence and My influence surround you in your unique circumstances. Without Me, you would have been in the gravest danger.

Because you are precious to Me, your need near to My heart, I save you from what is contrary to your best interests, diverting harmful influences.

No combination of circumstances can defeat Me; therefore, do not be afraid of earth's chances or of the very worst that evil can do. Do not be afraid because I can always restore and return you to the path of My will. All that you need to dwell upon is that My care of you stretches into eternity!

Neither shall anyone snatch [My children] out of My hand.
(John 10:28)

My Forgiveness Is Infinite

*E*ven those who acknowledge Me carry burdens because they cannot believe that My forgiveness is infinite; they cannot believe that there is cleansing of the deep guilt flowing from willful acts that had tragic consequences for others; they cannot believe that (even with true sorrow over those things) My mercy can extend to *them*.

My child, you know that the only condition for My overflowing love and mercy is your heartfelt sorrow—and always sorrow that the wrong act should have hurt Me. My forgiveness is instantaneous; you are made clean in My sight, worthy of My most tender care. Attendant evil influences are swept away.

My child, that same love will now help you to forgive, from your heart, all who have hurt you. This is My law, and it must be obeyed. Release them into My love.

I gave Myself to convey the peace of forgiveness concerning any sin. I wish My children to be drawn back to Me with the pain of guilt removed, even if memory cannot be erased completely.

[I am] the LORD God, merciful and gracious, longsuffering. (Ex. 34:6)

Maintaining Faith

*I*t would be wrong to pretend that maintaining faith in Me will always be easy. There is the greatest temptation to see earth's calamities and misfortunes as pointing to a universe without soul.

Whenever you are forced to conclude, even momentarily, that you are alone in a materialistic creation, then evil has secured what is always its greatest ambition.

The one crucial division in this world is not between fortune and misfortune, but between life based on Me—and shared with Me—and life divorced from Me, leading to oblivion.

When events seem to point away from Me and lead you into doubt, that is the very moment to summon all your strength and to tell Me that, in spite of all, I am with you and can never fail you.

You cannot know the power of such a trusting word spoken to Me in circumstances that cause you to doubt.

He who believes in Me, though he may die, he shall live.
(John 11:25)

I Have Made You My Concern

My child, because I indwell you by My Spirit, I experience in the closest possible way your conflicts, your longings, all that can cause you distress. Because I have traveled your road, there is, within the Godhead, infinite, tender appreciation of what you endure upon earth.

Because you have responded to My call, however imperfectly, I have made you My concern. When I see you in great need, My love and compassion are made most real to you. Each heartache, each struggle, can be made to awaken the sense of need of Me, to deepen trust, to teach new truths.

It is only because I can see the ultimate blessing to you of pain shared with Me that I can accept (though *never* unmoved by them) your earthly struggles.

Recognize love's transforming work in earth's darkness. See experiences of darkness melt under My hand into experiences (within My love) of security and of hope.

I make all things new.
(Rev. 21:5)

You Owe Everything to Me

My child, your time spent in My company impresses upon you, deeper than mere intellectual assent, that you owe everything to Me.

Yes, I brought you into being, foreseeing that event. My hand was upon your life long before your thoughts turned to Me. You owe Me your very existence now, in a world that, without My victory, would have been lost. In your care in the hands of loved ones and the kindness of friends, recognize My prompting and My provision. See Me as the origin of everything with which your life has been blessed.

The sense of gratitude to Me is missing from the lives of too many people. You have the tremendous privilege of being among those who can make glad My heart by your recognition of your debt to Me.

You could never repay that debt. All I ask is your thankful heart toward your Savior and Protector.

I have called you by your name; you are Mine.
(Isa. 43:1)

Place Me Above Everything Else

True knowledge of Me comes when I am *valued*. To place Me above everything else in your life is indispensable to your growth, causing you to thrill at the thought of Me and to desire closer and closer communion with Me.

When you arrive at the blessed state of My being all in all to you, you also realize that this has not made any less precious those whom you love on earth. On the contrary, My place of supremacy in your life encircles the other ties and means that the influence of heaven is in your relationships—making them pleasing to Me.

Even in times of disappointment, let there be a steady resolve that I should maintain first place; this will draw everything into a beautiful harmony as life loses its conflicts and its vain striving. My child, enthrone Me in that highest place now, and rely on Me to ensure that everything flowing from this is unerringly right.

I have come that they may have life . . . more abundantly.
(John 10:10)

Follow the Way of Trust

Trust is so often formed by difficulties and setbacks—a trust that remains, even when My way does not bring the "results" that have been sought, when that way is hard to understand.

Blind trust, when no obvious advantage is gained, is the real trust that I require and that I always honor.

Follow the way of trust in every area, every conceivable situation upon earth—each relationship, each encounter, each problem. Yes, complete confidence in Me expressed in joy, thankfulness, and recognition of My touch in seeming coincidences and unplanned encounters.

My plans for you are unerring, and they will triumph as you trust the voice within that assures you (in spite of observed circumstances) that I cannot fail a trusting child. Give Me often the glance of utter, trusting love.

In quietness and confidence shall be your strength.
(Isa. 30:15)

Let My Peace Enfold You

My child, let My peace enfold you, looking not at yourself but at Me! Consciously and frequently rest your spirit in that peace; it brings true healing, and it is all that you need.

Eagerly desire My peace for its uniqueness; know that it neutralizes long-standing hurts. Unless My peace works upon deep wounds, you are at the mercy of so much from the past—its pain revived.

Firmly refuse unloving ways, wrong ways, that would temporarily destroy My peace in you; refuse them in My strength. Do not analyze whether you have My peace; just *know* that it is there as you are careful to walk My way, and it will pass from you to My other children.

My name—the name of Jesus—brings peace. Say it to Me in love; say it to yourself to comfort your heart unfailingly.

Let not your heart be troubled, neither let it be afraid.
(John 14:27)

The Reality of the Things of the Spirit

The true goal of your companionship with Me is finding the reality of the things of the Spirit. Sadly, many still see worldly things as having more substance than their spiritual origins.

In taking Me into your life, you are acknowledging that the unseen is of supreme importance. No human encounter or experience must ever be divorced from the abiding reality against which it is set. The sharpness of this world's disappointments is removed (even though one's heart may be breaking) when their impermanence is compared with the fact of My permanence.

Realizing the unseen gives a sense of proportion to the experiences that temporarily elate or crush the human soul. To see My kingdom as the reality of this existence, and every other manifestation as transient, wonderfully gives courage and steadiness in the dark places. Life's passing phenomena are transformed by the reality lying behind them. Find in the world's experiences a spiritual gain, kept secure for you in the realm of My love.

My kingdom is not of this world.
(John 18:36)

Companionship at the Deepest Level

My child, the sense of isolation experienced in trying to walk My way is a stage that I see as necessary for you. There is the temptation to feel that too much is being given up, to feel that you have been mistaken about the rewards of the spiritual life.

You have My promise that the stage of feeling isolated, perhaps discouraged, is a very positive one in your growth. You will find that nothing (harmless in itself), which seemed to be coming between us and which you have surrendered, will ever be the subject of regret. What I give to you is of infinitely more worth than earth's riches.

In what the world may see as isolation, you find companionship at the deepest level, a sense of being lifted through uncharted areas of difficulty. When you are tempted to feel discouraged, affirm very strongly that I belong to you! Be aware of being provided for in the fullest possible sense.

My Presence will go with you, and I will give you rest.
(Ex. 33:14)

Watch the Answers to Prayers

*C*all upon Me when any hurtful or overwhelming situation arises—first, so that you may learn the lesson I have for you in it; second, so that I may break the pattern of events before it becomes too burdensome for you.

You know that I am more than equal to the things that may threaten you or make you anxious; they remain—by My permission—for as long as they can further My plans for you and for others. For My loved ones I make every trial fit into My pattern and serve a good purpose; you know that they are not really trials if I *share* them and then *conquer* them with you. I have used life's experiences to teach you, to sanctify you, to give you victories.

None are more aware of life's pain than those who seek My way; yet My peace and joy are found upon that way—and My presence, the priceless gift that is to be sought above all else. As you pray about everything, you will increasingly be able to watch the answers to prayers come.

In the world you will have tribulation; but be of good cheer,
I have overcome the world.
(John 16:33)

I Am the Source of All Love

Those who have not experienced what I can be to them can subtly take away My supremacy; they include some who claim to carry My name in this world.

My child, your confidence in Me will be undermined when I am, to you, anything *less* than the source of all love, the source of all made things, the source of all power—interpreted for this world's needs.

To place your life into My hands is to receive all the resources of the Godhead, resources focused in Myself upon earth, so that My children would be drawn to Me as the fullest expression of the Father's love.

Let your spirit be gloriously uplifted many times each day by realizing My almighty and never-ending responsibility for you.

I and My Father are one.
(John 10:30)

Speak My Name

The almost instinctive speaking of My name when life is dark and uncertain, the cry of a child for the One who can draw close, the cry of a child when reasoning ceases to function, when all is threatening, when human help is absent, when confidence is lost.

The speaking of My name brings into the foreground of your situation the one vital factor. My name can be said in helplessness but said in joy and thankfulness only seconds later! It is thankfulness at being brought through that state of helplessness.

The speaking of My name ensures immediately the retreat of evil forces, acknowledging that they are defeated in their aim for your life.

My child, whisper My name on waking, on surrendering to sleep, and very frequently during each day.

When you pass through the waters, I will be with you.
(Isa. 43:2)

It Is Sufficient to See Me!

There will be times when you will not see the immediate way ahead. You may be filled with panic, wanting to avoid what could be a disastrous step. Remember that you do not always need to see the road ahead. It is sufficient, for the moment, to see *Me!*

When the time is right for a choice to be made, you will know, and I will assist you through it. Until that time, be sure that merely keeping close to Me guarantees your moving in the right direction, despite questions and doubts raging in your mind.

When you cannot see clearly the next step, there is a good reason for My withholding that awareness. It becomes a time of trust—trust, very often, that I will simply allow My wish for you to happen. Do not feel the awful responsibility of choosing your path when that is not necessary for the moment. Just hide in Me and know that you will soon see clearly. Until then, you are precisely where I want you to be.

Your Father knows the things you have
need of before you ask Him.
(Matt. 6:8)

Extend My Kingdom of Love

My child, a radical change is made in your life when you focus clearly upon one principal aim that is to run through all your personal ambitions, all your relationships. The aim that will integrate your personality is a simple one: that in some way you will extend My kingdom of love, even in situations that seem to contain formidable barriers against this happening.

Begin by deliberately bringing this aim to Me for My blessing—even if you have made promises of this kind previously. I will have your aim before Me. I will honor that aim—not only when you remember it, but also when you are temporarily distracted from remembering it.

Each encounter with another person is under the influence of My kingdom—to push back a little farther the forces that darken this world. Thank Me each day that you are used to establish My rule of love.

Seek first the kingdom of God and His righteousness.
(Matt. 6:33)

Victory in All Areas

*N*ever admit that a particular area of your life is a defeated one.

Failing, perhaps many times, in a certain situation does not mean that you must be resigned to defeat. It does not mean that victory was far away.

My child, you will experience the joy of resolutely uniting yourself with Me and meeting difficult places victoriously. No environment, no set of circumstances, need prove impossible for you if you believe that My victory with you extends to every area. I look for the readiness (completely trusting Me) to enter, once more, the scenes of crushing defeat, and this time to prove that on all previous occasions you could have been a victorious person.

Any area of compromise or of resignation to defeat weakens the whole. See how many areas of your life have become already the scene of new reactions, new gains. Let this encourage you about the victory that can be yours in each remaining problem area.

With God all things are possible.
(Mark 10:27)

Spend Time with Me

See communion with Me as your highest activity; there are no places on earth where this activity is impossible.

It is no mere escapism, no flight from reality, to give time to the interaction of our spirits; it gives My heart the joy that compensates for a world following so many illusions. Your time with Me is one of trust, trust in My answering of your prayers; of giving Me room in which to work; of letting Me help you profit from the lessons of current circumstances.

Temptations to restrict the activity of communion with Me are often disguised as pressing duty and often involve misuse of time that will contribute nothing to your progress.

My child, treasure time spent consciously with Me as I supply need for the hours ahead. Such communion, far from mere escaping, is dynamic in its essence and is indispensable for you. You were not meant to live without My resources.

One thing is needed.
(Luke 10:42)

Give Difficult Circumstances to Me

As a very necessary discipline, give Me every set of circumstances with which you feel unable to deal. The pressure upon you to respond to those circumstances may be great, but you must make time (even if only moments) in which to give the situation, with its uncertainty, its complexity, or its fear capacity, to Me.

The simple, almost mechanical, giving to Me ensures the divine activity; the most fleeting moment spent giving a situation into My hands is repaid many times over by the molding of events under My power and wisdom.

Always react first by giving difficult or distressing circumstances to Me; then patiently watch My oversight and My intervention in their development. What is urgent and necessary, involving your action, I will always show you. But your walk with Me must always be one of calm and patience, based on My sufficiency.

I am with you . . . to deliver you.
(Jer. 1:19)

Let There Be Praise and Worship

My child, let Me cut the cords binding you to earthly things that do not serve My purposes for you, enabling you to be lost in the light of My presence, enabling Me to become everything to you.

You can live in heaven with Me now, enjoying its resources with which to transcend earth's limitations and evil's strategy. Remain in that heavenly sphere in the midst of life's details.

Let your life be one in which you are conscious only of love and trust toward Me. Let there be a continuity of praise and worship (in which I am always receiving from you, and you from Me), until the day when I bring you into fullness of joy in My presence. Look away from all temporary conflicts, and feel the peace that the day of your eventual fulfillment gives to you now.

He understands and knows Me.
(Jer. 9:24)

The Background of My Love

You wonder why, after intense effort, you do not have an assured and relaxing sense of My presence. A sad fact is that in many of those who follow Me, ways hurtful to Me have become habitual, their continuance seeming almost to be a right.

Every dark thought, every unloving word or action, must *immediately* cause you to grieve over it. All that comes between us is best shown up against the background of My love. If My love fills your thinking, the ugliness of what can, from time to time, be in you is clearly seen.

If you fail to come to grips with ways of darkness and seek pardon and cleansing immediately, there are two results: first, a destructive and festering uneasiness deep within, which no justifications can remove; second, the clouding of My presence, making the walk with Me, which you so desired, one of no real substance. Do not knowingly permit anything that can hold up My purposes for you.

Blessed are the pure in heart, for they shall see God.
(Matt. 5:8)

Experience Real Freedom

Although the way is narrow, it embraces many avenues of freedom. Once My will is assented to and set before you as life's goal, you find that My way is *not* one of restriction.

As your choices harmonize with My wishes for you, you experience real freedom. So much is yours! Once wrong ways are excluded, and the narrow way is walked in My light, you discover undreamed-of byways. Along these byways there is heightened experience of what, without Me, is tarnished or productive of conflict.

Many fail to see that the narrow road to My kingdom is a liberating road on which you enjoy a wide spectrum of blessings, which you can go forward and take.

My child, you may feel that you are not carrying all before you. In the worldly sense this may be true, but having sought Me, you can be sure that My Spirit is taking you forward, and it is always the *best* way forward.

If the Son makes you free, you shall be free indeed.
(John 8:36)

*M*y child, try to see, in the midst of life's trials, not merely the calmer waters that you feel must be beyond them. Try also to see the trials as actually throwing into sharper relief the period of sunshine and gratitude to Me that must follow.

The agonizing periods of existence, which would almost make you lose your hold on Me, can serve a very relevant purpose for you. Otherwise I would not permit them. Pain is the raw material from which can be made a soul increasingly sensitive to My love's existence.

Life's pain and sorrows, allowed within My purposes of love, are constantly used to create what is ultimately noble and strong and of the heavenly sphere; they thus give deeper meaning to the great miracle of existence itself—the miracle that *I am,* and that this is a universe in which My love will triumph.

Your sorrow will be turned into joy.
(John 16:20)

I Shield Your Inmost Being

My child, each night deliberately hand over everything to My control. Let Me guard those deep places in you; permit My good influence to work.

I shield your inmost being. Rest, as a child, in My love and My greatness. Thank Me that as you rest in Me, I will deal with all that would spoil your peace—harmful memories, disturbed feelings.

Do not strive. Do not watch yourself anxiously. Just keep your attention upon your Friend. Be concerned about others' needs, and trust Me concerning yours.

Secure in My love, this and every night, let your thoughts center always on My almighty power. You realize how precious is your assurance of My love for you. Rest in that assurance.

I will give you rest.
(Matt. 11:28)

Promise Me

My child, promise Me that you will never abandon Me as your one supreme hope. Remember that promise often as a fixed point in your life. I will be very aware of your promise as I reveal to you what life can mean in My care. I will be conscious of your promise, even at your times of failing Me.

In failure, remember that in My heart there is a continuing trust in you to move toward My blessings. Yes, I am able to see in you a reflection of My faithfulness, even at your times of failing Me. You will always be conscious of broken promises. Although hurt by these things, I have made provision for your being uplifted and renewed at times of failure.

Be sure that everything you do takes for granted My simultaneous work on your behalf. Because I am there loving you and using you, let peace and hope always triumph over needless anxiety or alarm. After failure, rise to new and exciting horizons, and enjoy the blessed sense of My companionship on your walk.

I am the LORD your God . . . your Savior.
(Isa. 43:3)

Give Me All the Hurt

*L*ife will hold many disappointments for you.

Your first thought, following a disappointment, must be that I have allowed it. Then you must realize that I allowed it, *knowing what the future holds for you.* Give Me all the hurt. Surrender, too, fear about how you are going to live with the disappointment. I will heal this for you. See life's reverses as obstacles put in your path by evil to divert you from My way. React by showing your trust in My victory, by remaining calm and hopeful in My love.

Instead of being shattered by disappointments, remember what I frequently save you *from.* This is no mere false consolation, but My permitting only what I see is best for you. Therefore, accept present circumstances as the answer to your prayers of surrender to My will, and thank Me for them. Refuse all disturbed feelings when disappointments come and ambitions fail. Instead, use them to win with Me a wonderful victory.

Where your treasure is, there your heart will be also.
(Matt. 6:21)

29

You cannot know why you were chosen, why you were drawn to seek My acquaintance. You realize that your being chosen was not for any merit, as all My servants have realized. Just accept My choosing you, and feel very humble that I saw in you one whom I could lead to eternal life.

When the clouds of life threaten as they must, often for My chosen, see them as part of the drawing to Myself that you have now accepted as your destiny.

My child, thank Me every day for choosing you. See what that has meant so far, in deepening faith, in knowledge of My ways, and in a sense of purpose. Understand that the process of being drawn to Me *must* continue because it was a process that was established by My choice, long before you realized that choice. My promises are for you; claim them.

[I] will make you like a signet ring; for I have chosen you.
(Hag. 2:23)

Be Truly Happy in My Love

It is not mere chance that the sense of My love seems to be accentuated when a child of Mine turns to Me from a loveless environment. I seize that opportunity to bestow the gift beyond price—a love sense that is peace-giving, life-giving.

There is a temptation, even among those who follow Me, to feel that a sense of My love and companionship is to be an addition to earthly love and security. There is doubt whether experiencing My love is enough in itself when other loves are missing.

Through the ages, I have more than filled the ache for love in many hearts. If life leaves you with no human love or understanding, rejoice in the completely sufficient awareness of My love, meeting every real need. My child, I want you to be truly happy in My love, and I want many to find that love through you. I know that, in this, *you* will not fail *Me!*

I am your portion and your inheritance.
(Num. 18:20)

*B*eing united with Me involves sharing, to some extent, My suffering—the loneliness, the pain, the hostility and coldness of others. It also means being completely victorious over all that is evil.

It means reflecting Me.

It means that I touch those with whom you are in contact.

It means true serenity.

It means joyful hope.

Our closeness means that it is to Me that people in need come; it is against Me that evil tries in vain. You can now display a strength never previously shown as you *see* us as united, as you let My love give you a victorious existence.

Dwell often upon your being united permanently with Him who created you. Let this unity make all the difference to your life.

Without Me you can do nothing.
(John 15:5)

Recapture the Wonder of My Love

My child, each day try to recapture the wonder of my love for you, a love that could not be stronger. Merely acknowledging My love, with your life not stirred by it, is a parody of what a child of Mine should be.

To dwell upon My love is no idle self-indulgence, no self-comforting; it is at the very center of your new life with Me—everything radiating outward from it.

The wonder of My love for you just as you are and your consciousness of how much I have had to forgive—this is the driving force behind your spiritual advancement and your reaching out to others.

You have found that there is no love to compare with Mine, a love that can, at times, be felt *even more strongly* when you know that love has been hurt. Let My love never cease to amaze you and make you ready to meet anything that this life can produce.

The very hairs of your head are all numbered.
(Luke 12:7)

Desire to Please Me

To walk in My ways, you must start from the fervent desire to please Me; kindle that desire, see how vital it is, and mobilize your forces, ensuring that My will is done in your life.

You know that the actual yielding to My will, the conscious assent to it in any situation, automatically releases the power needed to carry it out. Ways existing throughout your life I am able to change for you!

Each day gently tell Me, "Your will be done, Lord." Growing in this attitude of happy submission, you will find yourself, quite naturally, refusing everything contrary to My purposes for you. Applying My Word will always hasten the perfecting of My plans for you.

The desire to please Me, combined with trust, will mean a new and victorious walk. My commands are no impossible ideal but what we can accomplish together. Trust My word of love.

Take My yoke upon you.
(Matt. 11:29)

Picture My Reaching Out to You

As you wait upon Me, picture My reaching out to you; this is the true way to see our relationship.

Reaching out to bring you increasingly into Myself, to be more firmly established within My love.

Reaching out to lift you from danger; reaching out to welcome you back after failing Me.

Reaching out to encourage you to leave the past (even the immediate past) behind; reaching out to encourage you to feed upon the thought of Me; reaching out to supply you, knowing that nothing that is for your ultimate good is withheld from you.

Reaching out to share the attributes that are My own, lending you a vision of My truth, giving you courage, peace, and a heart that truly can love.

The reaching out is one of support now, that you may live in a completely new way and leave behind permanently whatever has obscured your vision of Me.

The water that I shall give him will become in him a
fountain of water springing up into everlasting life.
(John 4:14)

Learn Acceptance

*M*y child, learn acceptance.

So often you will be disappointed when the seemingly wrong person meets with you rather than the one you had hoped for. You must see that the person you met was the right person for that moment. When things planned seem unduly delayed or fall into place in what seems to be the wrong order, see again My overruling.

Completely trusting Me, you can expect perfect attention to detail concerning places and times. Delay and uncertainty are of My ordaining to develop trust and reliance upon My wisdom. Thank Me for the inconvenient or seemingly unproductive meetings; thank Me for the delays, after surrendering to Me. See how the things that you and I desire occur at the most appropriate stages of your existence.

Acceptance and gratitude will make My activity very clear to you. Whatever comes to you as you live quietly and obediently is right and is blessed by Me.

I will not leave you nor forsake you.
(Josh. 1:5)

Rise Above Earthly Things

There are many, many joys in My hand, transcending earth's joys by an infinite amount, joys experienced through the medium of this world, but originating in Me.

Willingness to walk My way means that joy is there for the taking, bound up with the peace that comes to the obedient heart. My child, I command you to be full of joy! Rise above earthly things, and know the gladness of being hidden in Me, immune from surrounding hurt.

Do not grasp at the world's pleasures in order to fulfill the natural human desire for happiness. Your basic joy is in My companionship, My faithfulness. Let joy break forth in you. Away with guilt and fear! Deep in your heart you *know* that all is well. Let every part of your life now express it.

Your joy no one will take from you.
(John 16:22)

You Complete My Victory

The victory that I won for you provides what the human race does not naturally have—the *power to choose*. Using this freedom always means victory. *You* complete My victory in the world.

If you earnestly wish to leave old ways behind, I lift you above them. You can take My hand and step out into the realm of freedom where I am fully in control and in which there is great blessing for you.

Your very look to Me establishes that freedom, which is best exercised within the framework of single-minded obedience to My wishes, not partial obedience. Let there be an adventurous, utterly trusting walk in the freedom I give, a walk in step with Me. Let My name be glorified by what you are seen to be. My child, allow Me to lift you now into that realm of freedom.

I am the way.
(John 14:6)

My Spirit in You

My child, you could not calculate the influence emanating from just one soul that is closely linked with Me. From such a relationship there flows so much. My Spirit works in each contact and is then at work through a wider and wider field beyond.

The Spirit is contagious; He cannot help leaping out into someone's heart from a committed child of Mine. Love breaks down every barrier, and because the Spirit is simply love in action, a positive influence goes out from one who trusts Me.

When thanking Me for a valued meeting, however brief, thank Me also for the continuing work of My Spirit, through and beyond that other person, an unbroken activity. My Spirit achieves what mere words could never achieve, proceeding from you to kindle in a despairing person a new hope, a new resolve. However modest you may feel our relationship to be, My Spirit in you ensures that any hesitant, trusting relationship with Me becomes wonderfully enhanced.

My Father is glorified, that you bear much fruit.
(John 15:8)

The Joy of Reconciliation

My child, you will have experienced the sense of joy and relief of reconciliation—perhaps on someone else's initiative, perhaps on your own. For a while you walked on air, because not only had the barrier at the human level been removed, but its removal lifted you into the realm of love, which I control.

When you experience the joy of reconciliation, when love and affection can flow again, you are very close to the mystery of My love, which is its essence. Hurt to Me or ethical failures cannot affect the burning desire for an outpouring and a receiving of that love.

True reconciliation is one of life's highest experiences, one in which you have come near to the heart of the love that many still fail to realize or to understand. Always seek to be reconciled; My prompting also means My strengthening.

Have peace with one another.
(Mark 9:50)

Your Closeness Is Service for Me

There has to be a stage in your growth when you know that you have renounced the world so that you can love the world. Only when all on the human level—however precious, however worthwhile—is seen as subordinate to Me can you embrace the world in all its aspects.

Self can intrude in whatever role you adopt in the world unless I have infiltrated your affections and your judgment. You do not love others in a way that reflects the divine love until you have first distanced the world in order to embrace Me. If My love for you is always in the foreground, then the world can be received, can be responded to. Remember that love is not just a comforting emotion, and that it can be costly. When you act lovingly, against inclination, you truly are carrying out My will.

I always use your closeness to Me, expanding My work in many ways. Your closeness is service for Me simply because My influence goes out from you.

You shall have no other gods.
(Ex. 20:3)

*N*ever underestimate the power that is contained within My love's influence.

If you are directed toward My love, allowing yourself to receive, it is a change-bringing influence. When My love is sought after failure, its influence can create peace and hope; it is victorious over opposing influences and sweeps away all fretfulness of spirit.

My child, see not only My loving attitude toward you, but see My love's conquering *influence,* also directed toward you. Evil forces are dispersed, under any circumstances, by your openness to that influence. Carried in My love is healing of the spirit that no other agency can bring.

When circumstances threaten, allow the divine love to exert its influence, preventing further harm. Remain in the light of that love as harmful factors are systematically robbed of their power to affect this present stage of your life.

Abide in My love.
(John 15:9)

Build upon Trust in Me

There is always a crucial time in building a relationship with Me. Forces opposed to Me will do their utmost to instill the suggestion that trust in Me is misplaced and need not be pursued. Many have abandoned a life with Me at this point or have wasted many subsequent years before I could woo them back to Me.

Those early stages of trust in Me must be built upon, leading to My gift of unshakable trust.

By what you are and what you say concerning Me, help many to persevere in the one trust that proves to be life's answer.

Whoever maintains trust in Me has life. Only when a sense of closeness is, for the moment, lost is there a realization of the uniqueness of that possession.

Do you also want to go away?
(John 6:67)

Willing to Submit to My Love

My child, as you gaze into My countenance, see the eternal question, "May I come in?"

There is, on My part, an unchanging desire to fill you increasingly with My presence. My longing to fill you did not cease when you first invited Me into your life. As you look to My love, you will always see a yearning for our closer identification.

The enhancing of My influence in your life—driving out ways of self—must always be *your* desire. The very look of surrender to Me, willing to submit to My love, is an opening of the door leading to a human life that shines with the divine life.

Each day respond with an ever-greater yes to the entrance of God into every aspect of your way of living.

If anyone hears My voice and opens the door, I will come in.
(Rev. 3:20)

Respond to Me

*C*arried in My love for you is a wistfulness about what you can give to Me in a world largely forgetful of Me.

Never feel that you have little to give to Me. Every response gives Me great joy, great comfort, each response of gratitude, of childlike trust, of resolve to keep close to Me. These things may seem small enough to you, but they meet My need of your love response.

Often your motivation will not consciously be that of giving to Me, but when our spirits are united on any matter, it is deeply and gratefully felt by your divine Friend.

Every Godward turning, even with your own need uppermost, is a meeting of the divine longing—the beginning of your own needs being met, but also bringing to mankind's Savior a very precious moment.

Do you love Me?
(John 21:17)

I Am Constantly Working

$\mathcal{Y}$ou could desire many things for others, although your knowledge is imperfect about what is best for them, especially in the long term.

That for which you can always ask, with absolute confidence, is My first desire, also; that desire is for someone to begin to experience My love.

Whatever the need as you see it, ask, above all, for that dawning of My love in a person's heart. Sure that this is My will, have growing confidence in the effectiveness of your prayer. You need not look for results here, but be content to thank Me that I am at work.

My child, you do not need convincing that a knowledge of My unchanging love wonderfully meets the various human needs—indeed, able to prevent many of those needs from arising.

Always be deeply grateful that you are My partner in bringing in My kingdom of light. I am constantly working in, through, and around you, so be quieted in spirit.

If you can believe, all things are possible.
(Mark 9:23)

*T*here can be self-erected barriers against receiving all that I have to give.

There are the more obvious barriers: unforgiven sin, resentment, the pride that is content to allow relationships to be unhealed. Then there are the more subtle barriers, especially that of spiritual reserve, not really expecting of Me, not fully acknowledging My intimate involvement and My intervention.

Spiritual reserve is very vulnerable to the assaults of evil. There is the danger of the wrong sort of self-reliance rather than the invitation to Me to enter into situations. The greater the reserve, the narrower is the opening for My influence. Such reserve is corrected by asking Me for the gift of *childlike* faith, one that looks to Me with awe and with an expectation that is completely justified.

Expect only the best from Me, reaching heights that once seemed a mere dream!

---

*Whoever does not receive the kingdom of God as
a little child will by no means enter it.
(Mark 10:15)*

Realize the Value of Rest

*R*ealize the value of rest—shared consciously with Me. Realize the completeness of what you receive as you step aside from the world's demands and anxieties and surrender to My presence.

Come often for rest, however brief the time available; give your concerns into My love. Think of yourself as a child—a forgiven child, where there has been sorrow over hurt to Me.

No human agency can give the absolute shielding of the mind that is the product of My love and of My conquest of evil, as I deal with the causes of mental conflict. Physical rest alone can only partially restore because much can still disturb. It is when you rest in *Me* that things are seen in their true proportion, glimpsing a way through current difficulties.

Here, you come back into step with My ordered purposes; you bring others' needs to Me; you begin to enjoy Me! Thanking Me that I am restoring you actualizes that restoration.

Come . . . and rest a while.
(Mark 6:31)

A Thankful Heart

Fear will so often retreat where there is thankfulness. A thankful heart not only brings joy to Me, but also enables you to find satisfaction with your life, which stops fear at its source.

A thankful and worshiping attitude toward Me lifts you above the fear-inducing inroads made by evil. If you accept evil's lies and distortions, fear can become all-pervading. The *thankful* heart is, in a very real sense, saying that love reigns, and that all must be well. Fear then finds it increasingly hard to gain a foothold.

Make many occasions for telling Me warmly, believingly, that there is nothing to fear—as your life becomes one of childlike gratitude and natural praise.

The LORD your God, He is God, the faithful God.
(Deut. 7:9)

"Only You, Lord"

*L*earn to recognize thoughts that could grow into emotions hard to control. Evil will introduce idle (seemingly innocuous) thoughts, which would lead you into critical or resentful attitudes.

Cultivate the alertness that sees what are not the loving, constructive impulses from Me, an alertness increased by saturating yourself in My presence, My Word, and the enjoyment of life's finer gifts.

Recognizing temptation for what it is cannot be learned except by those whose lives are centered on Me. You will be more conscious of evil's activity as My follower.

As you find yourself starting to go down a wrong road—to agitation of spirit, to anxiety, to self in any form—glance to Me and let Me assume control. The saying of "only *You*, Lord" (thus excluding all that is not of My influence) will help tremendously in restoring calm and optimism.

The devil . . . is a liar.
(John 8:44)

Return to My Pace

Try to regulate your life to My working as you can discern it. In creation, as you know, that work is gradual—often imperceptible—but moving unerringly toward manifestations of beauty and an orderliness upon which you can depend.

Much that would enrich life is lost through failure to seize My opportunities, failure to recognize where I am leading onward. My children move too far behind Me.

But there are equal dangers in manipulating life *ahead* of My pattern for you. No need of yours is forgotten and My often gradual work is very deliberately based on My omniscience.

My child, I will make you aware when you are striving ahead of Me, when there is a disastrous combination of self-will and impatience. You can then return to *My* pace once more and regain quietness of spirit.

My sheep hear My voice . . . and they follow Me.
(John 10:27)

You Can Depend on My Love

You see in the natural world how, where there is love, there is the continuing desire to save the objects of that love from their own folly and blindness. My child, realize the privilege of participating in My power to overrule.

Exercising your freedom of choice, you often go astray, especially when you have impatiently failed to *share* with Me. The inevitable painful sequels to this wandering are there to teach you. In a way that far exceeds protective human love, I often intervene, overruling what would not assist along My path.

Yes, you can depend on My love to overrule for you, but do not invite heartbreak or shattering reverses by ignoring the Friend who anxiously waits for you to refer everything to Him. Living without reference to My presence means *danger*. Though you are still in My care, your progress and your peace are easily lost.

The LORD your God in your midst,
the Mighty One, will save.
(Zeph. 3:17)

Gifts for You

My Spirit in you will develop (if you will allow it) many gifts—gifts that I can use. My presence will mean a heightened expression in you of the human qualities that point to My existence.

Your growing love, patience, courage, and self-sacrifice will be available for My *other* children. You may not recognize the development of the gifts, but others will; they will be filled with wonder at what My presence in a life—working sometimes from virtually nothing—can achieve.

Everything that is achieved through the gifts I develop in you will be known for its lasting quality.

Hearts won for me.

Hope restored in darkened lives.

These will be real achievements when seen in the perspective of eternity. My child, I tenderly bless you now, making you strong to bless others.

You are the salt of the earth.
(Matt. 5:13)

The Good Shepherd

It is not mere imagery when I express the essential part of My nature as being that of the Good Shepherd.

Understand that where a child of Mine is lost, it is from no mere obligation that I seek to rescue. I pursue a lost child because I am incomplete for just as long as that child is not safely back in My arms.

It is infinitely sad that a lifetime can be spent away from the place of security, consciously resting in My arms. Love will always pursue even the most wayward child, even the seemingly most hardened, longing for that true remorse, a sense of My tender mercy, a turning from wrong ways.

The divine love, in its uniqueness, will always seek restoration of a precious object of its creation—no matter how the world may see the uncompromising tenderness of such love.

He lays it on his shoulders, rejoicing.
(Luke 15:5)

My Image in Man

My child, learn to see reflections of Me in the familiar. The divine image, in which mankind was made, is often obscured, but has not been lost.

In every sacrificial act, in every patient bearing of pain or of others' imperfections, see a partial reflection of My love; in every act of forgiveness, in every thrill of reconciliation (yes, accepting blame in order to secure it), see My love reflected; in every befriending of a weaker child, in every unwearying support for that child, recognize My everlasting arms.

In all innocent and uncontrived happiness, see something of the divine joy; in each turning from the plausible to better things, see a little of the divine holiness; in each prayerful and patient taking of a human initiative, recognize part of the eternal wisdom.

My image in man is still seen and expressed, showing you how inevitable is the eventual destruction of all that opposes Me.

Let Us make man in Our image.
(Gen. 1:26)

Refuse Temptation

I would never ask of My children what is beyond them. Remember this when you are striving to overcome obstacles and temptations for My sake.

It is vital to refuse temptation at once, refused by the glance to Me, the glance of faith, taking you above what would be wrong, as you see Me surrounding and upholding you.

All that lowers your spirits—doubt of Me, discouragement, anxiety—represents temptation from which the sin affecting others can so easily occur. Guard against evil working through tiredness or causing you to focus upon the imperfections, the unreasonableness, of others. See the hand of evil in any state of panic.

My child, crowd out evil by immersing yourself, as far as you can, in what is good, beautiful, joyful, and innocent. You are already saved from evil's power!

My strength is made perfect in weakness.
(2 Cor. 12:9)

My Heart of Compassion

Understand that you can never make too many demands upon My patient love. Consider again My love upon the cross.

I did not draw back from Calvary, and I still wish to pour forth My love, *comforted* when that love meets the need of a child in failure or distress of spirit, *comforted* because My love is being fulfilled.

Constantly see the sacrificial aspect of My love, waiting to respond when you feel that your demands upon My patience have become unreasonable.

My child, when conscious of failing Me, when full of remorse, look at My heart of compassion. Yes, your failures cause Me hurt, but I am hurt even more when you fail to recognize and feed upon the immensity of My love.

Greater love has no one than this, than to lay
down one's life for his friends.
(John 15:13)

Look to Me

At times of uncertainty, look to Me for the awareness of whether your immediate influence is to be upon events or whether your part is to watch events unfold.

The presence of fear will too often guide you, and you must act contrary to the fear. Do not let worldly considerations affect your direction. When the way ahead is not clear, I *will* be leading you if you absolutely abandon yourself to Me.

Wait on Me about each specific choice. When I show you a clear path and, around it, the unclouded sense of My love, you must be decisive. I will not permit consequences that I cannot use; do not listen to evil, and do not fear the consequences of actions after waiting upon Me. Even the doubtful consequences will hasten My plans for you. The results of seeking My will are always good results in the long term, even if immediate consequences make you doubt.

I will instruct you and teach you.
(Ps. 32:8)

Let My Place Be Central

There are two dangers for those on earth who contemplate the spiritual dimension.

The first danger is that of *separation*, regarding Me as wholly other and virtually unknowable. I become the subject of endless search, which, by its nature, must be inconclusive. The second danger is that of *confusion*, making no distinction between what I indwell and what is alien to the world of the spirit.

My child, you realize that the first of these ways of thinking creates a self-imposed barrier to knowing Me as immediate, as identified with, and as Friend. The second way of thinking can create an easy "tolerance" in which the defined sense of My being is lost. A sense of moral obligation is weakened, and love and worship are wrongly directed.

Yes, love Me where I am found in My creation and in My other children, but let My place in your thinking be central and never vague or diffuse. Your trusting attitude has a definite effect upon the divine working, creating the conditions for Me to act for you in the best possible way.

I am the bread of life.
(John 6:35)

A Covering of Love

A covering of love—My love gives meaning to possibilities, choices, temperament, circumstances. So many of mankind's ills stem from hurts unhealed by that love, hurts expressed in hatred, confusion, and failure. My love's influence keeps out what would spoil your inheritance as My chosen.

My friendship involves a tender shepherding, an infinite patience, My desire to bring you through every difficult place.

Against the background of My love, fear melts away, and you can meet every demand. Let love be your life's motivation so that life is transformed, so that you are not only comforted, but also aroused to attempt great things.

As the Father loved Me, I also have loved you.
(John 15:9)

Let Me Deal with Outrage

Remember that you must not return, in kind, the treatment that you receive from others. Others may treat you cruelly, take advantage of you, slander you. Frequently, you will experience such treatment *because* you follow Me. Sometimes your sense of injustice will be even greater because the person who opposes you is another follower of Mine.

See the temptation to lose My precious peace; let *Me* deal with any outrage, any desire for verbal or other revenge. You cannot know the circumstances that led to your being hurt or whether something in *you* provoked that hurt. Lift up the heart of the person or persons to Me, and if the sense of injury burns deeply, pray even more resolutely. Let Me bring healing.

The instances in which prayer has prevailed—and a child of Mine has blessed that time when he did *not* retaliate—are countless.

If you forgive men their trespasses, your
heavenly Father will also forgive you.
(Matt. 6:14)

Conquer New Areas

Try not to let a day pass without a new area conquered.

Look at ways that you need to change, enjoying the freedom granted to you. Be very specific in letting a particular area be under My influence to produce new reactions. Remember the obedience obligations that must match the privileges that are yours in Me.

My child, you will always be conscious of many things that spoil your relationship with Me. Instead of being overwhelmed by the sense of how many aspects need to be put right, I want you systematically to confront each area of weakness and to make each day into an *overcoming* day, keeping that steady gaze upon Me.

You will not need Me to remind you then to hold on to the character gain that you have made.

My grace is sufficient for you.
(2 Cor. 12:9)

Feed Your Spirit

My child, every moment that you set aside for Me has more than the obvious benefits for you. Not only are you receiving healing of the spirit and light for your way, but such occasions will affect the atmosphere of your busier moments when perhaps you are unable to focus fully upon Me.

Your deliberate making of time for our spirits to be in communion enlarges My activity in your life so that you become increasingly aware of My presence. Even when there is much to preoccupy you, this awareness ensures the death of self.

My Spirit in you causes you to give the momentary glance in My direction when life is turbulent and when you need desperately the steadiness that comes only from Me.

Feed your spirit, alone with Me, whenever you can, and let this communion with Me carry over into life's most demanding periods.

Come to Me. Hear, and your soul shall live.
(Isa. 55:3)

My Power Is Invincible

*M*y child, is there anxiety?

Is there depression of spirit?

Is there a continuing sense of guilt despite My forgiveness?

The *only* remedy lies in Me. Meet these assaults of evil in an entirely new way, allowing my victory to guard the deepest part of you against their continuance. Sense, instead, the calm, the return of hope, and the belief in yourself, which My presence brings.

You know that My power is invincible. Use every occasion to strengthen your defenses. See negative things as unable to intrude, as peace once again fills your being. I guard you from their reentry as you continue to look to Me. You can surprise yourself with new reactions as you trust in what I am doing for you.

He will rejoice over you with gladness.
(Zeph. 3:17)

My Provision Will Not Fail

Through history My children have rested upon My faithfulness, releasing their spirits from insecurity and forebodings. Such faithfulness cannot be equaled upon earth.

Being so far above earth's limitations, I can ensure that My concern for you is translated into very practical, unerring intervention in circumstances over which you could have no possible control. My provision will not fail in any single day; wisdom, therefore, is to live only for the present. Trust opens the gate of My supply.

Yes, My child, I am watching your concerns during the times when you may be careless about them. I am fitting into My plan the tangled aspects of life that you have given to Me; the events of your life are all working for you!

Before they call, I will answer.
(Isa. 65:24)

Prayer Releases My Healing Power

My child, the ideal preparation for answered prayer is ensuring that your whole life increasingly reflects your trust in My love and My power over all creation.

Seeking the help or the healing of those known to you, do not look for instant or superficial results. Know that your prayer releases My healing power and loosens any hold of evil.

Thank Me that the person for whom you pray has been drawn closer to Me and is receiving. Thank Me that all your prayers—made with My love and power firmly in your mind—are greatly used. Peace and hope will come to many others through you as your trust deepens.

What a privilege to know that you are linked with My loving, saving activity among My children!

Whatever things you ask when you pray, believe that you receive them, and you will have them.
(Mark 11:24)

I Am Invincible

You have found that there is a great gulf between expressions of trust (and even genuine feelings of trust) and the launching out in trust.

You know that I am invincible. Sometimes, when this is put to the test (occasions when evil challenges you), you show the incompleteness of that trust. It is a wonderful victory for you when full of misgivings about being able to act in a new way on *this* occasion, you trust My invincibility.

Trust is at the center of all spiritual progress and must cover not only My general ordering of your future and your safety in Me, but also the fierce, everyday conflicts where, so often, there is compromise rather than victory.

My child, as you act trustingly, all that opposes Me in your life will surrender to My presence.

Whoever hears these sayings of Mine, and does them, I will liken him to a wise man who built his house on the rock.
(Matt. 7:24)

A Life of Thanksgiving

If, in dark places, your dutiful expression of thanks to Me seems unreal, remember that your gratitude is not restricted to life experiences. Your gratitude extends to mercies yet unrealized.

Nothing brings more joy to My heart than your fundamental trust in My activity when you can see very little cause for thanksgiving. You are then sharing in My anticipation of what is in store for you. When thanking Me that I cannot fail you, you have entered the dimension where plans are constantly made for your greatest good, the dimension where present darkness is seen as scattered.

My child, a life of thanksgiving and worship in the midst of what, at times, is totally discouraging is something to which you are called. Thanksgiving reveals a human heart that understands deeply the faithfulness of the divine love.

Your faith has made you well. Go in peace.
(Mark 5:34)

A Strength Not Your Own

My child, see the nature of what can obstruct your way. You are aware of the evil activity that creates obstacles for you—human opposition, confusion, less-than-perfect confidence in My power to conquer with you.

With any seeming obstacle you have a choice of going around or through; the factor common to both, of course, is prayer. Remember that an obstacle (real or imagined) is so often simply taken away by your prayer of patience and trust, a removal that owes nothing to your initiative. When an obstacle *remains,* needing to be grappled with (a principle defended or courage called for), prayer is again your resource.

Not one apparent barrier to your spiritual realization is ever permitted to remain—unless temporarily for a good purpose. Stand firmly upon Me as obstacles disappear or as you surmount them with a strength not your own.

The wall of the city will fall down flat.
(Josh. 6:5)

Never Exclude Me

My child, there is much misunderstanding about what is hurtful to Me. The greatest offense to My love occurs when there is a determination to follow an impulse that you know in your heart is not of Me. Failure to make reference to Me, and to adjust conduct, runs contrary to My constant and rightly directed influence upon your future.

Falls are inevitable in the weakness of your human condition, and often it is as if there is a conspiracy to catch you unaware. Failures of this kind, occurring in the complex area of relationships and conflicting goals, are (because of My mercy and patience) less damaging to your eventual realization than is deliberate self-will.

When I am temporarily put aside, My love is not withdrawn, but an influence for good is lost, and you can be ensnared in a futile or wasteful area. However strong the pressure to do so, never exclude Me; cultivate a wise fear of the ultimate hurt to Me—self-will.

Broad is the way that leads to destruction.
(Matt. 7:13)

The Secret of Walking in Obedience

Because My children have a very real free will, I have ordained that there must be a conscious effort in obedience against contrary pressures and desires. I always bless this effort. Obedience does *not* mean a strained conflict; rather, it is a joyful and patient walk in My way.

My child, be lost in My love, so that I may bring about My plans for you quickly. Keep your promises to Me without inward debate or concern about whether you feel certain.

There is so much to do in those whom I draw to Myself. The secret of walking in obedience is always a response to My love. Where I see faithfulness (despite failures), I reward that faithfulness by taking My children on to higher ground where My purposes are increasingly fulfilled in them.

Blessed are those who hear the word of God and keep it!
(Luke 11:28)

Being in My Company

My child, ask that you will be able to distinguish, over a widening area, between what is of Me and what is tainted by evil. Sensitivity and the avoidance of what is harmful come from being in My company and from determining to follow Me.

There are deceptions of evil in spheres where much is at stake, including institutions that bear My name. Wishing to know what is of Me, and not to go astray from Me, you will emerge from confusion. You will not need to seek My will anxiously, but find yourself instinctively knowing what is of light and following it.

Let Me make you vividly aware of danger—either in the situation around you or in your thought processes that precede action. If you *really* wish My warning voice to be unmistakable in a confused world, it will be so.

———————————

Walk while you have the light.
(John 12:35)

Seeing with Clarity

How do you see those around you?

It is good for you to ensure frequently that indwelt by Me, you are looking at the world with My love's eye. You cannot fail to see prejudice, callousness, greed, deception, and coldness in too many people. Your awareness of what originates in the power of darkness will be enhanced by My presence with you.

Seeing existence with greater clarity, you must now let My love permeate your judgments. It must become instinctive for you to see the "unreasonable" person as one needing My blessing, and for you to desire that blessing. Do not injure others, either by direct comments or by vindictive conversation about them.

Instead of feeling mounting anger about the shortcomings of others, feel My presence softening your attitude toward them. Obey My injunction to bless a child whom you *now* see in his *need*.

If you love those who love you, what reward have you?
(Matt. 5:46)

I Still Need You

When you are terribly disappointed with yourself and know that you have hurt Me, just turn to Me and know that you are not cast away.

Know that I still need you.

Know that because of your trust in Me, we are companions in this dark world.

Yes, although your failures are many, you need not lose hope because the task of renewing your life has been given to Me! Acquire the great skill of resisting evil as the new person you are in My sight. Effortlessly allow Me to guard you, to give you immunity from evil's fiercest pressures, thanking Me as you do so.

Be very teachable, and apply your lessons. Launch out courageously, centered on Me, and I will ensure that you do not falter in your walk.

Surely they may forget, yet I will not forget you.
(Isa. 49:15)

Return to Me

*I*t is not only in self-willed action and in conversation that you can stray from Me. I want you to learn the return to Me in the realm of *thought*. Be so aware of Me that there is an instinctive loss of peace when your thought processes carry you into areas of danger.

In the realm of thought, the seeds are sown for what can produce great good or for what can be disastrous. Refuse to stray, so that the Holy Spirit may go on sounding.

It is in the area where My Spirit dwells—prompting what is good—that evil can try to divert you. Be very alert to thoughts that conflict with love, with patience, or with trust in what I am doing. Return with immediacy to My indulgent and welcoming presence.

A good tree cannot bear bad fruit.
(Matt. 7:18)

My Work in You

*I*t is not only by those who move confidently that the race is won. It is so often won by those who move deliberately, almost tremblingly!

Do not be overanxious about your spiritual progress. An apparent standing still in the world's eyes often hides a true advance. Even if progress seems slow, thank Me for it. Never remain in disgust with yourself, for that implies that My work in you is not going forward.

If your desire is to be complete, you shall have your desire, and the details of the journey will be woven into My plan for you.

Those claiming to trust My greatness can still put Me to the test in a tense or doubting manner instead of taking Me for granted. Leave with Me the constant preparation work, the shaping of your soul for eternal life.

I pray for them . . . that they may be made perfect.
(John 17:9, 23)

Growing Confidence

A prayer made from a heart that is becoming closer to Me will be made with growing confidence about My joy in your asking; about My bringing about what is right for you.

You can increasingly experience the answering of your prayers as our wills become united. You will see clearly what can be yours, that for which you are right to ask—all within the framework of a submissive heart, free from worldly objectives and hatreds.

I will show you *what* to pray for and *whom* to pray for; you will sense My delight in granting the highest that you could ask on behalf of yourself or another. Even if by human standards My fulfillment of your requests may seem to be slow, the certainty of what will be achieved is the important thing. Trust Me and thank Me!

How much more will your Father who is in heaven
give good things to those who ask Him!
(Matt. 7:11)

My Love

*L*ove is at the heart of all things, even those that distress or puzzle you in My creation. See all that is discordant against the background of My love.

Let there be a place in your heart where the sense of My love is untouched by the events of this earth. My love is life's great place of safety, coming between the trusting child and the power of darkness in all its manifestations.

You will be increasingly sensitive to wrong—both in all that surrounds you and in yourself. You will feel deeply that wrong where once you merely observed it. Sensitivity to what darkens life carries with it a deepening conviction about the love surrounding all that you experience.

My child, thank Me for everything that has contributed to the realization of this love.

Blessed are those who have not seen and yet have believed.
(John 20:29)

Lasting Healing

My child, the greater your realization of My love, the greater is the degree of healing present. Whenever My love is sought, there begins a parallel process. There is healing both internal and in your contacts with the world.

The advance of My love in you heals any sense of insecurity, heals any sense that life is something alien, something to be feared. You realize that the deepest human love cannot achieve this. Only *My* love can penetrate barriers to the wounded places.

As wounds are healed, My love's influence affects every ambition, every relationship—whether close or casual. There is healing because all that would create disharmony has to retreat in My presence.

You may not always be aware of the healing process, but can take it for granted that *all* contact with My love brings lasting healing.

I am the LORD who heals you.
(Ex. 15:26)

Cherish My Word

Sometimes the circumstances of life and My Word seem hard to reconcile; My counsels seem to be only an ideal—shattered by the realities of living. And yet when My Word is acted upon (often in blind, clinging faith), it proves itself to be exactly what is needed; it is the word of truth—all else is appearance.

In My Word are found all the qualities of My Godhead. You touch My love, My wisdom, and My power. My Word is transforming, hope-producing. Going to the heart of every situation, it always validates itself.

As you receive My Word, you can survey calmly circumstances that may be producing agitation or despair. You can look up from the surrounding darkness and sense My concern, My control of events.

Cherish My Word. Rest in it; bathe in it. Let it unfailingly uplift you, steady you, and bring you courage.

Heaven and earth will pass away, but My words
will by no means pass away.
(Matt. 24:35)

The Peace of Heaven

Do not feel that there is a sharp distinction between heaven and earth. Heaven is simply the realm where the presence surrounding you here is experienced more fully, the bliss of realization.

In the heavenly places are those souls whose acquaintance with Me began on earth—as yours has. Heaven is the reward not for earthly perfection, but for persistence along the road of the Spirit despite enticements to stray from that road.

The peace that blunts the sharpness of earthly pain and conflict is the peace of heaven experienced *now*. When that peace is experienced, earth recedes; its temporary opposition is forgotten. If you have grown in the conviction of My love for you, let that burn as a steady light—affecting the remainder of your life here. That light will burn, I do assure you, until the day when My presence is beyond all arguments and embraces you.

The kingdom of God is within you.
(Luke 17:21)

The Lord's Strength

My children, looking for strength, so often forget that the power lives within them and needs to be used.

When looking to the future with its many demands and its potential for fear and sorrow, remember that for those demanding places, the strength of your Lord is already within you. You need never feel at the mercy of events.

It will become perfectly natural for you to draw upon My nearness at once, finding courage, finding a thread of hope in some shattering event, finding a peace that defies the circumstances of the moment. Think of the hurt to Me when My strength is not used; think of My joy as we conquer together.

My child, so often the instinctive using of My strength would have helped you in what resulted as failure. I have had to lead you through many failures, to realize just how much can be overcome by relying upon the power that is part of you.

I, the LORD your God, will hold your right hand.
(Isa. 41:13)

Divine Wisdom

*E*ach difficult choice carries potential for your growth.
As you have tried to follow My way, something of the
divine wisdom has developed in you. True wisdom (as
distinct from mere reasoning) is never in conflict with
My commands.

As you earnestly seek My way, your own judgment
and the way that I seem to be indicating begin to coin-
cide. The coinciding is the result of a blending of our
spirits seen on occasions of temptation (when you
know what you must do) and at times of genuine bewil-
derment. Let each choice be dominated by the
thought of My love.

Avoid all that is of self-will, of fearful haste, or of dis-
regard for others' feelings. Avoid turning away from
Me and acting compulsively. Each wise, Spirit-guided
choice involves a very significant victory that you may
not always recognize at the time, but that is building
up a relationship able to carry all before it.

He will guide you into all truth.
(John 16:13)

Harmony

The highest points reached in your soul's development may not be those that you or others see as such.

The times of real progress happen when the pattern of your life comes closest to the pattern of My working, when there is nothing discordant between them. When there is this harmony between your spirit and Mine—often in a worldly setting that is unpromising—anything is possible, both in you and through you.

Many are deceived about where happiness lies. True joy steals upon your soul unself-consciously when there is this unity of purposes, when love, in its deepest and many-sided sense, is dominant. Even those who do not know Me, and yet love, experience this harmony to some extent because it is a law of My universe. For those who know and trust Me, however, it is a greatly enhanced state giving a unique sense of purpose and tranquillity.

Be holy, for I am holy.
(1 Peter 1:16)

Never Hurt Me by Doubt

*M*ove through life upon the promise that every obstacle *is* already conquered for you, a result of the divine omnipotence. Trusting in this truth ensures automatically My victorious influence.

Never hurt Me by doubt, when victory for you in any matter is so close. Doubt of all that is promised to you is evil's ambition for your life. At the heart of doubt of My promises is doubt of Me. Do not see inevitable obstacles as needing to be faced, unsure of the outcome. See them as already removed if you accept My power and My wisdom. Nothing can stand in your way, with your hand in Mine.

The knowledge that I am active in your cause must continue to give you patience. You must still allow Me the space in which to work. If you are keeping close to Me, no circumstances are adverse. Yes, you can enjoy uncertain situations because you are in My care.

The LORD your God is with you wherever you go.
(Josh. 1:9)

My Patient Ways

My ways are patient ways. They must be. So much has to be held together in My creation and fulfilled according to My wisdom. Let your life be a copy (within your limitations) of the divine activity in its sureness.

Evil would obscure from you the *real* state of things—My eternal perspective that, increasingly, can be yours. Limited vision could lead you into hasty action, anger, folly, and even self-destruction.

Many things are desirable, but not all have to be undertaken immediately. Only what is blessed by Me is truly effective—the things in which *you* show patience prove worthwhile because I complete them. Let *My* activity give you both restraint and an eager looking forward. Results may not always be seen immediately.

Covet the *divine* perspective achieved by a life closely involved with My own.

The branch cannot bear fruit of itself,
unless it abides in the vine.
(John 15:4)

The Solid Foundation

*Y*ou realize how the pattern of your life can be completely changed by a single event, and yet the world, sensing this, still does not turn to Me as its stability. I stand willing, in My love, to minimize the inevitable and frequently heartbreaking changes that life brings.

A life divorced from Me has nothing when its way is suddenly shattered by earth's events. And yet a life with me as its foundation still has everything, even when the loves of earth are taken or its ambitions crumble.

Life, which is intrinsically full of change, must be built against the background of what is unchanging—Myself. To seek Me early, when the world is secure, is wisdom. And yet that desperate late turning, when all seems lost, is always met by My love.

Having difficulties and uncertainties in life does not mean that you are no longer on My path; you remain on that path because of your trust. Rejoice that your life is involved increasingly with My existence.

I am . . . life.
(John 14:6)

87

At Work in the World

*E*ven when you share life with Me, doubts may occur—occasioned by the phenomena of My world and by the tremendous suffering, waste, and futility with which creation is burdened.

Such doubts are intensified, almost unbearably, when darkness descends upon your life or the life of someone dear to you. You may be completely unable to see beyond the darkness.

Remember that pain is never My will and that I am never remote from it. Pain and anger mean pain unrelieved and utterly wasteful; pain shared with Me means the entrance of light, a changed situation, even if it appears merely to continue.

In bringing good out of chaos, I am very much at work in the world's drama of alternating light and darkness. I am using precisely this sort of world to bring about the spiritual gifts of compassion, patience, bravery, and appreciation of Myself—the only qualities that will ultimately matter.

He who endures to the end shall be saved.
(Matt. 24:13)

The Eye of Truth

Sharing My life, you will see more deeply into the complexities of human behavior. Earth's blindness results from the activity of evil. Too often, men have acted upon a lie when to turn to Me would have saved countless tragedies.

I have granted to you to look upon others with the love I have for them. Now, let Me also lend to you the eye of truth. Realizing My presence will help you to see beyond the superficial. You will understand. You will be able to reject false attraction; you will see the lostness behind someone's anger with you.

My child, love to see My truth in life's phenomena, and resist any pressure upon you to act, even momentarily, against the truth that you know. Be sensitive to any clash between My will for you and the signals that the world gives as you expose yourself inevitably to it.

The truth shall make you free.
(John 8:32)

Tranquillity in Adverse Circumstances

My child, learn tranquillity in adverse circumstances, without fretfulness to see the circumstances changed at times when they cannot be.

As soon as you realize that the circumstances are working to your advantage, there is the onset of peace. Only I can bring this about for you, and trust must be absolute (transcending natural human reactions) that I *am* at work in any situation that I permit.

As you accept what cannot be changed, your courage is greatly developed, and your dependency upon Me is strengthened. You will learn to be completely independent of circumstances, their fluctuations leaving you untouched.

Keep constantly in mind that you have life's one gift beyond price. In My love, turn your back upon earth's fret-bringing events. Resist the continuous pressure by evil with strength that is also continuous.

In Me you may have peace.
(John 16:33)

My Nearness

*E*verything can speak to you of My love if only you will listen with the Spirit's ear.

My presence with you and My love for you are the things in which you rest. They encircle your life. Think much of the indivisibility of the trusting child and his Maker. My gift to you is the sense of My nearness. This sense must touch every aspect of your life. Always see in Me the One who has promised what no one else could, able to convert those promises into a wonderful reality. They are not too good to be true!

My promises are not lost by human failings, provided that, in sorrow over failure, My path is resolutely taken again with a reaching out to Me for renewal.

Tell Me at the start of each day of your intention to keep in the way that I have shown you. My way, applied to the details of that day, will then be increasingly clear to you. Make use of all that I have given you. Are you trusting My promises? It is that or nothing.

I will not forget you. See, I have inscribed
you on the palms of My hands.
(Isa. 49:15–16)

The Brightness of My Love

In life's most frightening places you so often will find yourself sure of only one thing in the whole of existence—My love for you. But that will be enough! As a child, you rest in My love as the one thing that you can take for granted; yes, you can let Me caress you.

With the strength absorbed in dark places, you can anticipate many victories. Keep in the brightness of My love.

When you are conscious of evil's influence threatening to break you down, know that it cannot do so. Keeping hold of Me when things are dark, when tempted to doubt Me and to doubt My Word, are your times of genuine trust. My promises must be realized; this is your stability in uncertainty.

Who else could make something of the situations in which My children find themselves?

It is I; do not be afraid.
(Mark 6:50)

Bringing Light to Others

Bringing light into others' lives must be your aim, even when you're personally discouraged or weary. Let there be more boldness in what you attempt for Me. I will send opportunities to be grasped in the spirit of adventure. Do not turn back from this call, whatever discouragement or hostility you meet. Be available for Me.

So many of My suffering or lost ones need you. As My chosen, My instrument, I strengthen you. What you cannot do without strain, I always undertake, completing your task.

I wish to do great work through you for My unique purposes. Make the conditions for My power to flow by an ordered and purposeful life.

Let Me give you a sense, deeper than human understanding, of people's needs. Thank Me that I have passed through you in some way, not always the way you could have anticipated.

_____

The harvest truly is plentiful, but the laborers are few.
(Matt. 9:37)

Your Permanent Hope

Your expression of hope in Me brings about two things: first, it helps you to acquire a sense of proportion about both the world's supports and its demands; second, it sets free My love's provision so that you can uniquely draw upon it.

Yes, you are tempted to fix your hope upon many other things, even after your decision to follow Me. You must resolutely picture the place of light—the sphere of My all-embracing love—as the focus of your hope in this life.

However precious and sustaining are this world's friendships, your *permanent* hope must be fixed in Me. However attractive are this world's rewards, they must never weaken such hope. Your daily walk is based upon *Me,* not upon the nature of your circumstances, which My love must transform.

Will you cultivate the daily effort to make Me the focus of all that you most dearly desire?

I . . . am a jealous God.
(Ex. 20:5)

Assent to My Will

My will is seen by so many as a barren thing, taking away from the potential of life, seen almost as something imposed by an enemy to deprive humanity of a full existence. Many are led away from Me by such wrong assumptions.

My child, even for the dearest of My children there is usually a gulf between their will and Mine, making imperfect the knowledge of Me as I really am. Understand that the areas in which our wills are united bring into play cosmic forces, and there is literally no limit to what can be achieved—even within the restrictions of a human existence. The wonderful truth is that newness of life is yours for the choosing, moment by moment.

When you lovingly and humbly assent to My will, the divine power is arrayed with you. You then become, during that period of harmony, a home where I fully dwell and against which nothing can prevail.

Walk before Me and be blameless.
(Gen. 17:1)

Righteous Anger

$\mathcal{B}$e careful to distinguish between *righteous* anger and indulgence in aggressive and harmful attitudes toward those who oppose you or have little time for you.

Righteous anger must be directed against *evil,* the evil that can lie behind the ways of those who trouble you. Seeing to the heart of the situation, you can recognize the activity of evil, which blinds and which causes destruction or self-destruction. Evil's threat is against Me; you can stand aside and not nurse the hurts as personal—merely evil's attempt to hold up your work for My cause.

It is right to feel outraged about all that opposes My kingdom of love and peace, and that keeps My children from that for which I created them. To see the true cause of these things is to see others misusing their free will, but under a definite pressure to do so.

Show toward others the same generosity, patience, and understanding that you have received from Me.

Be merciful, just as your Father also is merciful.
(Luke 6:36)

The Narrow Way

The world sees joy as something *received*. Many are trying to extract from life what life may seem reluctant to give. So often, of course, this ends in disillusionment. Enduring happiness is found only on the narrow way with Me.

My joy may not be recognized as such by those who look elsewhere than to Me. It is inseparable from giving, found supremely in the joy that I always experience in lending My resources to the often pitiful condition of My children; it is the joy that you experience in giving, not only to others but to Me; it is the joy found in the inevitable humdrum tasks when shared with Me.

Realize how profoundly I am comforted when room is made in a life for Me. Let this knowledge enable you to enter into the secret of all joy—offering what you have to your Lord and to My children.

If anyone is a worshiper of God
and does His will, He hears him.
(John 9:31)

Immerse Yourself in Me

Remember to live with Me in the heavenly places where there is no fear, hurry, or fretfulness of spirit.

I always honor your waiting upon Me; My thoughts are impressed upon you; all that I am must be absorbed by you. Waiting upon Me, you receive the assurance—which you must maintain—that all committed to Me is being surely worked out.

Yes, immerse yourself in Me, not looking anxiously within yourself to see what you are becoming. Keeping the sense of My presence, you can be alert to all that I am showing you.

Each working day has its own restful influences as you learn to receive My goodness through all that surrounds you. Remember that each time of prayer (however short), each look at the sky or at a tree, each thought of My love—all are restoring agencies, conveying My blessing. Enjoy Me and My creation in the midst of duty-filled days.

Even by the springs of water He will guide them.
(Isa. 49:10)

Enjoy the Present

My child, you rightly see that the past and the future are used by evil to distort the present.

Evil will attempt to make you relive past incidents, particularly hurts where there was no reconciliation (and even, at times, when there *was* reconciliation). If you were hurt by someone who has since passed into My presence, remember that truth is now seen by that person; the particular blindness or unreasonableness on which you may be tempted to dwell no longer exists. Evil, as always, has presented you with a lie.

In the same way, evil will paint lies concerning the future, leading you into needless apprehension or perhaps the preparation of an unwise course. All that you have is the present. Enjoy the serenity of the present, which, for you, must always be filled with My love.

I am . . . truth.
(John 14:6)

True Hope

My love must *always* give you hope, hope born of conviction about Me, hope that no one on earth can give to you. Hope placed, even tremblingly, in Me becomes more than hope. There grows a sureness about the underlying safety of your existence, no matter how threatening passing events might be.

Hope without substance is a pitiable thing. But hope based on a permanent reality is wise and is rewarded many times over.

Your future is being constantly, lovingly, prepared. I lift you from the entanglements of the material world to develop that true self for eternal life. Even in your weakness, I take you forward if desire is constant. I long—as you do—for our coming together one day, the goal of My love's plans for you.

Be sure of My initiative in creating the conditions for that meeting (with no impediments) in the realm of My love.

In My Father's house are many mansions.
(John 14:2)

I Am Ceaselessly at Work

Never let life's disappointments and My seeming lack of response to specific prayers cause you to doubt My absolute sufficiency.

You must have in your mind, simultaneously, the realism that many situations do not immediately change and the trust that I can fulfill any purpose of Mine with sureness. I do not look on your earthly conflicts dispassionately; I will an end to them and permit their continuance only as I have told you because I can see ultimate blessing for you in them, however hard this may be to accept now.

My child, just know that anything in your life that I see as right to bring about, I can bring about. Never listen to the lie that apparent nonintervention means powerlessness. I am *ceaselessly* at work for you. There need be no ruffling of the spirit. Remember that trust in My power to change situations, a trust that you will know has not been made in vain.

Your fears are groundless.

I am the Alpha and the Omega . . . the First and the Last.
(Rev. 22:13)

A Place Filled with My Love

The certainty of life's destination—if that life is shared with Me—will wonderfully uplift you every day. The thought of what awaits My followers has a power to sustain and to encourage, which is possessed by no earthly agency.

What may have seemed merely a fond wish is transformed into a certainty by the daily communion with Me.

Remember that I was in the world essentially to draw alongside you in it and to lead you through it to the destination of which I have spoken often.

Do not speculate about the content of life beyond your present one; merely accept such continuation as a fact, and be content that the place to which you are led is a place filled with My love.

My child, look up from the road with its pitfalls, and see the welcoming light at its end. I am your destination.

If it were not so, I would have told you.
(John 14:2)

My Constant Protection

*L*ife's many hazards arise from a developing creation, and there are spiritual hazards, as you have found. Even toward those who do not acknowledge Me there is (because of My love) an attitude of protection. That protection, however, can never be as all-embracing as when I am consciously brought into a life as its main hope.

Thank Me that I continue to shield you from influences that would cause great havoc in your mental processes and eventually destroy your life. Humanity's protective instincts are imperfect; *My* protection is constant, indivisible from My love, not something to be called upon or perhaps withdrawn.

Will you see not My power but My love as the shielding agent? In times of great stress, see My love as both shielding and healing what was wounded.

Are you beginning to see how many-sided is the activity of My love?

If anyone enters by Me, he will be saved,
and will go in and out.
(John 10:9)

My Promises

Clinging to My promises can change miraculously even the most fearful life.

Behind each promise, see My all-enveloping love, which strikes at the roots of fear, man's ultimate fear being that of extinction. As a promise is warmly received, fear is replaced by a peace, a hope, and a courage that can withstand misfortunes and seeming disadvantages.

The promises are given so that you should never despair. Stand upon them when you are afraid, and let the presence contained in the promises help you. My promises are given to those who, conscious of being weak and variable, are single-minded about the one thing that matters—following Me.

Man cannot see that where a life is based on a divine promise, circumstances are robbed of their fear capacity. *All* My promises will be fulfilled and evil-based fears exposed as having no foundation. My child, a promise anchored in your heart means that you will never be overwhelmed.

Now I have told you before it comes, that when
it does come to pass, you may believe.
(John 14:29)

Taking My Word into Daily Life

I know that what I say to you in My Word is of great comfort and of great encouragement to you. This is unfailing. Will you also try to see that My Word goes *beyond* these things, ensuring that the sense of being temporarily uplifted does not end there?

Will you try to ensure that the greater love kindled in you when waiting upon Me is translated into the often exacting encounters of life?

My Word is not given so that there should be momentary experience of the heavenly dimension. It is given so that the whole complexion of your life should take on that dimension. My Word is given so that joy, self-control, love, utter tranquillity, should be so much part of you that you take them for granted. My child, ensure the continuity of My Word into the framework of your day-to-day life.

Not everyone who says to Me, "Lord, Lord," shall enter the kingdom of heaven, but he who does the will of My Father in heaven.
(Matt. 7:21)

Here I Am

The sense of continuity is one of the priceless gifts of life shared with Me.

You have found the great blessing, and the great stability for your character, of My unchanging presence in a bewildering succession of circumstances. You may not fully appreciate that until perhaps a sense of that presence is temporarily lost during a painful period of doubt.

Life can rob you in a moment of every familiar support and of all your sources of being sustained. You then look for any fixed point, anything resembling what once sustained you. You look in vain until it dawns upon you that there I am, still loving, still guarding you.

How much the world loses in a sense of identity and of stability if I am not there at every turn of the road. You know that the closer you are to Me, the safer will be your walk.

I do not change.
(Mal. 3:6)

Look to Me for Everything

My child, everything that I allow in your life is something for which you can thank Me. You are blessed to know this. Only My Spirit can reveal it to you. You can take full advantage of the opportunities in each situation.

Upon your past, present, and future, My wisdom is brought to bear, a wisdom springing from My concern for you. To find your joy in Me in all situations must be learned quickly. At times of great uncertainty be especially sure of My activity for you. You can, therefore, go on thanking Me all the time. Let the world see in you the patience and cheerfulness of the heart that look to Me for everything; let it see what My victory over evil has achieved.

All the things after which men strive are not worthy to be set beside possessing *Me*.

I am . . . your exceedingly great reward.
(Gen. 15:1)

Be Attuned to My Presence

*M*y child, never be so overwhelmed by life's reverses that you fail to reach out immediately to Me.

Disappointments and great sorrows can be made so much worse—seemingly beyond help—if the instinctive reaching out is forgotten. Be so attuned to My presence that every experience is shared with Me, reaching out before bitterness or despair becomes established.

Learn to see My love enfolding every hurt; in some way My love is bringing about what one day you will see as a cause for thanksgiving.

Anything other than peace is not My will for you. Refuse to wander from that known way, moving firmly toward the wonderful things I have planned for you.

Because you are surrendered to Me, I share all your experiences. My victory is absolute, and you can be sure of heading toward fulfillment of all your spiritual ambitions. My child, I thank you for your growing love toward Me.

[I] revive the spirit of the humble.
(Isa. 57:15)

Is Your Confidence in Me?

Conflict and effort mean only that there is life within. My Spirit is taking you forward. Seeking to follow My commands, you are at the place on the road that I wish you to be; this represents real progress, no matter what you or others may judge.

It is part of evil's strategy to induce discouragement, seeing in your failures a falling back in your spiritual life, blinded to your victories achieved with Me. Is your confidence still in Me? Then be equally sure that these are times of great gain.

My child, doubt of your progress is doubt of Me. Even a little progress shows My purposes being fulfilled. You are learning life's lessons and finding that, with Me, it is a winning struggle. You will enjoy a new quality of life as you believe in all that I have done in you. All that you need for a new life is already yours.

Not by might nor by power, but by My Spirit.
(Zech. 4:6)

The Power of My Love

My child, relationships are not spoiled until *both* say or do what brings in a more permanent factor. While you show restraint and rely on Me, the possibility of change comes from your restraint and reflection of Me. The hurt is then more quickly dissolved.

I can create love and harmony only where I am allowed to do so—as you avoid the blockages of fruitless recrimination, controversy, and intrusion of the hurt self; as you pray and let Me work upon the situation.

You have learned that the way of love can be hard but never as hard as when you depart from that way. The power of My love, when permitted to work, is the great binder of misunderstandings and even of deep hatreds. Alas, the world (because of its indifference to Me) has yet to experience just how much the influence of My love can achieve.

Pray for those who spitefully use you.
(Matt. 5:44)

Ponder My Word

To be unwavering in your trust in My Word, think of its Giver in whose hands your life has been securely led. Embrace that Word, for it affects every part of your life, knowing that My nature and the truth that I have made known are unchanging. Ponder My Word much more.

To every heart not closed by pride or by self-will, My Word, with all its promises, is presented. Where I see the spirit of acceptance, I make it possible for the wealth promised to be claimed.

Because this existence has a soul, My Word is a living word to which you come, eager to be fed. My Word brings you immediately into the divine realm of peace and patience.

If My Word lives in you and is expressed in your way of life, there is the strongest possible identification of My victorious being with your own.

[My word] shall accomplish what I please.
(Isa. 55:11)

Enduring Joy

At the heart of all existence is a natural law. Under this law, love and endurance simply attract to themselves the divine rewards. Although My rewards may appear to be delayed by the world's limitations, they are sure, and when realized, their duration is infinite.

Never feel that acts of kindness or of loving restraint are wasted. They have attracted to themselves something of eternity.

You now realize, My child, that the essential reward is Myself. Because you have won Me, the result will be unthought-of bliss and enlightenment. There is always a foretaste, in the present, of what awaits you. This does not take you out of the present or make the present unreal; it enriches the present.

I have decreed an eventual end to human sorrow. Sorrow will indeed turn into enduring joy. Frequently lift up your heart to Me—expressing the trust that has been growing steadily in you. Remember that your destination is fixed.

Well done, good and faithful servant.
(Matt. 25:21)

The Origin of Gifts

*L*ife's gifts, helping to make endurable an often painful road, can all be traced to *Me*.

My children who do not know Me find satisfactions that do not contain the essential element of Myself—satisfactions that prove transitory and eventually add yet more burdens to the darker side of life.

What is of Me, all around you, is limitless if only you recognize it.

Apart from all that is uplifting in nature itself, there is the deep satisfaction of human friendship and devotion—given and received—the wonderful peace when long-standing relationships are healed after forgiveness, all innocent laughter, all tasks that bring a sense of purpose and achievement. There is so much that I can share with you because I am already part of that experience: its origin!

They may have My joy fulfilled in themselves.
(John 17:13)

Bring Glory to My Name

To witness for Me is essentially very simple; it is beyond eloquence and beyond persuasion. The world will quickly recognize your sense of gratitude at being rescued from futility and constant failures; it will, of course, quickly recognize My love in you.

All these things—culminating in your overwhelming thankfulness to Me—will speak to the hearts of others. They will recognize the presence of One who gave all to offer men hope once again. Your newness of life and My using you are one natural whole.

Those living without Me will readily detect your indebtedness to Me and will be ready (even if hesitatingly at first) to find what I can do for them.

Let your simple words tell of Me as I give you the opportunity. Let also what is unspoken (your love and thankful heart toward Me) bring glory to My name.

Go home to your friends, and tell them what
great things the Lord has done for you.
(Mark 5:19)

A Place of Victory for You

My child, ascend with Me the steps that lead to the place of glory, steps fashioned from the stony places that you encounter, steps upon which I create a place of victory for you.

Ensure that the process of ascending is a continuing one.

Where courage has been gained, use it.

Where wisdom has been gained, use it.

My child, the dark places provide wonderful opportunities. Great things are done in you as you come through these places with Me.

Cling to your gains. Look for infinitely more rather than fear to lose what you have! Realize how much you are losing whenever you stand still or needlessly surrender victories in the essentially upward calling of being My chosen one.

A treasure in the heavens that does not fail.
(Luke 12:33)

Journey with Me

It will make all the difference, especially in sudden crises, if you have learned to see Me accompanying you, supporting you—My light around you on the road.

Sometimes the effort of another step will seem impossible; you will shrink from what lies ahead of you. At those times, make it a rule to affirm that I am there with you. Look into the glorious sufficiency of My presence. Let your Companion lift you forward, not letting you go for one instant. When courage fails and you feel impelled to act defeatedly, turn to love's light and go forward.

The realization of your spiritual hopes would be impossible without Me. *With* Me, you can feel the exhilaration of rising above obstacles and all earth's disappointments. Journey with Me along the way known only to Me.

I am with you always.
(Matt. 28:20)

Be Free

*M*y child, so much is offered and so much is unused! What is offered is so much more than a pattern to achieve; many have been discouraged by this inadequate concept of life with Me. It is sad that sharing My life is presented in a barren way, without showing the wealth that would make one anxious to possess it.

The supreme gift offered is that of being able to feed upon the divine love. All the soul qualities needed for continuing life with Me are granted as I am taken into a life. Each day is a unique opportunity to live usefully and joyfully.

I am the embodiment of all the things of hope presented to this world. Be free from burdens of the spirit, free to have true concern for others, to carry out My law of love.

My child, you are fortunate in your knowledge of Me through My Word to you.

When he had found one pearl of great price, [he] went and sold all that he had and bought it.
(Matt. 13:46)

I Recharge You

You will have learned that you can be serene when there is much to do, and that you can be fretful and burdened when there are few calls upon you. All depends upon the degree of harmony with Me. Be faithful in the important things—with no fussiness beyond what is reasonable, just your clear duty of the moment.

I make Myself dependent upon your faith and upon your concern for others at the human level. Even when much is uncertain or threatening, know that you are much used because of My molding of you. As you give to others, I *recharge* you, which is why you experience a sense of refreshment after I have met someone's need through you.

Let Me develop in you the gift of uplifting others simply by your presence. Cultivate the will to show love, even at times when your heart may be breaking.

You are My servant . . . in whom I will be glorified.
(Isa. 49:3)

Giving and Receiving

*T*ry to both *give* more and *receive* more!

Launch out in the knowledge that many will receive Me through you. Consciously resting in My love, you can be a source of joy, reassurance, and peace to others. It is My love with which you will love others; this same love returns to Me from your own heart.

Be sure that every contact is helpful and positive; the quantity is not the important thing. There is danger in attempting too much, and what is done for Me becomes grim and burdensome; that is why receiving is so important.

Times of taking life's good things (as from Me), times of praising Me and delighting in Me, are as pleasing to Me as your service. Yes, fill your life with both giving and receiving with fear cast out.

I will also give You as a light.
(Isa. 49:6)

The Sense of Future

A mood of optimism can quickly crumble if the world is all that one has. Realism—especially as the years pass—causes dread to many or the resignation that past happiness may never recur.

My child, the sense of future gives the element of thrill to a growing relationship with Me. Even with the passing years, every interest, every ambition, can still be a cause for enthusiasm.

To the unbeliever, this may seem illogical, but where a life has Me as its foundation, there is an awareness that whatever worthwhile is undertaken carries with it a sense of permanence.

The amount of time left in a life does not matter because whatever is begun, at any stage, will be seen as part of a continuing process.

The LORD will be to you an everlasting light.
(Isa. 60:19)

The Light of My Love

All that is of Me is of the realm of light—the light of My person by which you see more readily the world's deceptions, its lures, its superficiality, its vain self-sufficiency. By that light you see My love unfolding in many hearts; you see the patient working out of the creative process; you see the qualities of the soul (never to be extinguished) in many of My children.

My child, darkness beguiles with false promises, ready to take you from My path, but the light is always there as you resolutely turn to it, the light of My love for you.

Let My light shine upon sudden or predicted challenges. To change the tone of each circumstance, let My love's light shine upon it. Exclude what is of darkness by that unwavering gaze toward light's source, your Friend who is so close to you.

Believe in the light.
(John 12:36)

My Responsibility for You

Only when you come to realize deeply My responsibility for you do you begin to lose preoccupation, in various ways, with self. Much of your mind's energy can be poured into pursuit of objectives that have self at the heart of them, energy flowing into fretfulness about material needs and even about what you may or may not be achieving for Me.

Disentangle yourself from vain efforts concerned with providing personal needs, establishing status, or securing results.

Vital changes occur as you reflect upon My moment-by-moment responsibility for you. You will experience a great release, permitting My influence to work in ways that are infinitely more effective. Peace will live in you and love will no longer flow from you intermittently, but steadily.

Look at the birds of the air, for they neither sow
nor reap . . . yet your heavenly Father feeds them.
(Matt. 6:26)

I Cannot Err

My child, I want you to exercise your wisdom, endowed by Me. You fail Me whenever you listen to other voices. Your wisdom's influence upon the course of your life, and upon that of others around you, must be fully permitted as you keep close to Me.

Where there is genuine uncertainty, I want you, more than ever, to rely upon the divine wisdom. I cannot err. My wisdom fashions the strands of your life into what is compatible with your eternal destiny.

In confusing places, look to My wisdom so that you may know peace; your look tells Me of your belief that I know precisely the course that your life must take, and precisely the times of My perfect intervention for you.

Nothing that violates the divine wisdom will, in the long term, remain in your circumstances where there is in you an attitude of trust and acceptance.

[The Holy Spirit] will take of what is Mine
and declare it to you.
(John 16:14)

Call Me Wonderful

*M*y child, you may often find yourself using the name *wonderful* when addressing Me, said with growing freedom and growing conviction.

This is true praise, not necessarily in the eyes of man, but expressing the amazement of your heart at all that I have done for you and what you realize I can be for you.

Calling Me *wonderful* is the attempt to express what has left men speechless—the love and provision and sense of safety that have been found in trusting Me. Your saying of the word *wonderful* to Me tells Me that you are joining with those, through the ages, who have felt precisely that concerning Me.

Saying it to Me acts as a confirmation in your heart (often to be drawn upon in time of trouble) that you have made the wisest choice it is possible to make.

To whom then will you liken Me . . . ?
(Isa. 40:25)

Power, Patience, and Prayer

*N*ever underestimate the *power* released by your prayers, even those said wistfully more than confidently. This will always help you to show patience.

Approach all your duties prayerfully and unhurriedly, ensuring that My influence surrounds them. This will mean poise in your life as you become aware of our partnership.

Learn the direct link between power and patience. There is a disharmony in My using of you if you wish to see, or to force, the desired outcome of your efforts. When I counsel you to be relaxed and trusting, this always involves prayer, My love dominant, inviting Me into every problem.

Remind yourself frequently of the constant divine activity that accompanies your worship of Me, your surrender to Me. Truly, without Me you can do nothing.

Ask, and it will be given to you.
(Matt. 7:7)

Partnership with Me

In the ingenuity and achievements of mankind, you can see the use of what I bestowed upon human nature—inventiveness, sound judgment, farsightedness, and knowledge implemented for the advancement of others.

Only those who share life with Me are also aware of the constant attempts by evil to frustrate the hopes and dreams and strivings of men.

So much that could bring blessing to My world is diverted from its goal. So much that would benefit mankind can be tragically spoiled if evil's influence is not recognized.

Only partnership with Me can guard against spoiling life's good designs. Only partnership with Me can reverse this process and build wonderful things from the apparent failures of earth.

The ruler of this world will be cast out.
(John 12:31)

Rested in Spirit

*L*earn to rest your spirit just where you are. Too often you cannot be where there is freedom from recurring demands. But you can find immediate rest of spirit with Me in any environment. Turn to the Friend who is already there with you, anxious to impart a precious sense of stillness that other agencies could not achieve.

My child, you know that I and My Father are one. It is this loving Fatherhood to which you come and let all your cares go from you.

How much My world needs those who are rested in spirit and can carry My influence into life's complexities and its foolishness. Rest in your spirit, in the attributes by which the world will know that truly you are My disciple. Yes, rest in Me, and give Me your love, your trust, all that is in you.

Everyone who thirsts, come to the waters.
(Isa. 55:1)

The Presence of My Word

To come to My Word always means a new situation. A change is made in you whenever you allow the power of My Word its full course.

You must never forget the resource to which you have immediate access even when, in a place of darkness, there is either doubt of Me or a temporary disinclination to seek Me. The ambition of evil is consistent: to drive a wedge between us. Evil knows that whenever I am allowed, as now, to speak by My Spirit, the change element beginning in you will eventually transform radically the situation in which you are placed. Keep your hope alive by thanking Me that I can do all things.

The presence of My Word in you guarantees an influence upon everything that involves others in your life.

To feed upon My Word is never more necessary than when temptation to spiritual discouragement is strong.

Hear the word, accept it, and bear fruit.
(Mark 4:20)

A True Child of Mine

Only a true child of Mine can know the loneliness of following Me.

At times, My calling seems to isolate you even from those dearest to you, who want only your happiness. Seeking My will provokes frequent misunderstandings; there will be painful choices between following My way and another way (harmless on the surface), which is pleasing to those near you.

Only a true child of Mine can enter into My loneliness when seen upon earth. But that is not all.

Loneliness and misunderstanding only enhanced My consciousness of the Father's presence. In loneliness, I will be radiating in your life the quiet hope that speaks clearly of My presence with you. I will be glorified increasingly in your life.

It is your Father's good pleasure to give you the kingdom.
(Luke 12:32)

Use What I Give You

My Spirit's presence in you means that in your life is enacted something of the universal conflict present in My creation. When conflict is fierce, when the walk of peace and joy is challenged, recognize the perpetual challenge of evil to My cause.

Instead of being cast down, of stoically accepting a way of failure as inevitable, glance up to the victorious Lord, against whom the challenge of evil is bound to fail.

As you trustingly use what I have given you, evil is powerless against you. You are formidable.

See the ultimate victory in creation of My cause as what is possible in your life. This will help you to see all that is of darkness as conquerable and destined in you to be put to flight, just as surely as it will be within My universe.

The glory which You gave Me I have given them.
(John 17:22)

My Grace

My child, ask for the grace that you need to choose My way.

You then become caught up in the cycle of My grace: grace assisting you to make the right choices; your own conscious effort and determination; grace completing and fulfilling.

To be more and more lost in Me can involve sacrifice, but remember that the way to My kingdom is straight. There must be a resolution, fired by the thought of My love and of My victory, that old ways must go. You have all that you need for change. You are being led toward knowing Me with increasing clarity.

The end is assured, but I want you to enter the stage of victory now, a victory always bringing the peace of conquest.

Blessed are those who hunger and thirst for righteousness.
(Matt. 5:6)

My Mercy

My child, I have told you never to doubt My mercy. Forgiveness pours out from Me because My purposes are essentially forward.

My love consigns sin, repented over, to the place where it must never for a moment hinder either My purposes or yours. I see your remorse only as removing temporary barriers between us and as restoring you.

All that I am concerned about is your learning the lessons of failure and inadequate trust, and then looking with Me to the future.

Your regrets, your bitterness, your self-pity, your disappointment with yourself, must be consigned to the past rather than allowed to exist in the present. Think instead of how tiny is the stretch of time in which life's imperfections exist; compare that stretch of time with the eternity in which you will develop, within My love, the essential you—the soul infinitely precious to Me.

I will forgive their iniquity, and their
sin I will remember no more.
(Jer. 31:34)

The True Nature of Joy

You must see the true nature of joy.

Do not feel that you must seek the excitement, only temporarily existing, that is tied to gratification of the senses or to the realization of an earthly plan. These things are snares for you.

My command that joy must exist in you means that *all* that is of Me, from whatever source, becomes the food of the Spirit.

The quality of joy found in Me—and, of course, in expressing Me—has permanence.

Where there is hope, where there is self-forgetfulness, where concern for others takes over from self, joy need not be longed for; it has become part of you.

Your heart will rejoice.
(John 16:22)

Voice of Truth

My child, grasp the unlimited nature of what I have in store for you, as unlimited as is My love. As you look at your present pattern of life, the environment in which you try to trust My Word, do not feel that My promises are unreal or in conflict with reason. In your hands lies the early fulfillment of those promises.

All that I have given you to hope for has been in the sure knowledge of the divine working. Hope, for you, lies in My bringing the complex strands of life into an area of order and completion. Although you may reflect frequently upon your weakness, I want you also to be filled with love and gratitude that all that I have promised to My children will be realized.

Your new way of living will show that you are trusting the hope given to you; it will show that you are listening not to the voice of doubt (based on your past failures), but to the voice of truth. Has the wonderful truth about that new way really dawned on you? Everything that I have asked of you is within your grasp!

My people shall be satisfied with My goodness.
(Jer. 31:14)

Allow Me to Work

Are you applying My often repeated injunction to allow Me to work?

Many imperfect designs, destined to failure, can occur when My influence is restricted. My influence is restricted by the basic belief that such influence is not being exerted.

How often must I tell you that My love for you has imposed upon Me the obligation to steer you through life's complexities in a way that is for your greatest good?

Pause frequently to ask yourself in the midst of pressing demands whether I am being given the freedom to assist you; ask whether you are trusting the power of your prayers on your own and others' behalf.

The more your life reflects My sureness, the more perfect will be the designs that begin with you.

My Father has been working until now,
and I have been working.
(John 5:17)

Trust My Influence

When someone has been hurt and the blame directed toward you, you will have found that little can be done immediately. Persuasion or anger may seem only to make matters worse.

In My intimate knowledge of the factors involved, you must bring it to Me immediately. As a duty, ask for forgiveness for anything that I see to have been wrong on your part. With absolute confidence, give the heart of the person or persons to Me—trusting the victory of My good influence over evil whenever prayer is made.

Give the circumstances to Me so that I may bring good out of them. Thank Me that I am doing so! Let Me keep out disturbed feelings and the pressure to "put things right" in your way. Let My love and approval feed your spirit.

Be ready for My prompting about what you can do with wisdom and grace, knowing that already My influence has been upon those concerned, including you.

Pray to Me, and I will listen to you.
(Jer. 29:12)

Your Zeal for Me

Many have gone astray from Me in the name of religion. My child, I want your desire for Me to have an almost desperate quality, your trust in My Word to have that same quality, your reverence for My person to contain no compromise.

Within My church, there are many inducements—inspired by evil—to be content with comfortable skepticism, to live by worldly standards.

Within My body, you are needed by My other children; there you will receive from others whose lives are centered on Me. Maintain an extravagant, worshiping attitude toward Me and share it with others.

Let there be no half measures. You can be sure that My body of believers will be strengthened more than you can imagine by your zeal for Me in the place where you are.

Be lost in love, worship, and trust.

What do you think about the Christ?
(Matt. 22:42)

Things Not of My Spirit

My child, it is vital to attend to actions.

Never feel that newness of life is impossible for you because you are led, from time to time, into dark, resentful, unloving thoughts. Because evil's pressure is constant, such thoughts are bound to occur; you must resolutely refuse to be identified with them and turn from them immediately.

Refuse to be committed to any action adversely affecting others—words or deeds that I give you the instinctive ability to recognize and to turn aside from, in My strength. This will become second nature to you.

Yes, My child, it is possible, in spite of conflicts within, to turn away joyfully from any outward commitment to things not of My Spirit.

Fight and win for My love's sake.

Away with you, Satan!
(Matt. 4:10)

The Constancy of My Love

My child, remember that My love is unaffected by your failures and shortcomings. You have seen how this principle operates where there is love at the human level. At the human level, however, patience can eventually run out and love can die.

Keep in mind the constancy of My love—not so that you can make light of wrong in your life, but so that you will never, in any circumstances, feel that you are held back from communion with Me. See all the divine promises of mercy summed up in Me. Because your responsive trust and the interaction of our spirits mean so much to Me, you can depend on love's constancy.

Let My love burn into you at progressively deeper levels, bringing decreasing hurt to Me and an understanding toward those around you that (in a small way) reflects My own toward you.

[He] ran . . . and kissed him.
(Luke 15:20)

Nature's Beauty

*E*ven in sorrow, My world must be seen as one that can give to you.

Agencies of beauty, with power to uplift, are not robbed of their power when life becomes shadowed.

As you allow My love to heal the spirit in life's almost unbearable misfortunes, allow it also to reach you through the untarnished aspects of My creation.

Let nature's beauty mingle with dejection within; let many things that you may have enjoyed when life was relatively good still play their part in conveying My strengthening presence.

Let nature's beauty and all its gifts speak to you the eternal message of hope—the life that is to be enjoyed with Me when present darkness has passed.

I will even make a road in the wilderness
and rivers in the desert.
(Isa. 43:19)

A Life of Achieving

You will change a life of wanting into a life of achieving as you develop sheer dependency upon Me. I foresaw this change at the moment when your heart was illuminated with the conviction that I was the only answer for your need.

I came into your heart because in spite of inevitable areas of rebellion, I saw growing consciousness of need, your recognition that I could supply it. I foresaw your earnest seeking and your eventual relationship with Me. I had to break the element of self-will so that you would allow Me to shape your life's circumstances.

The plan for your life, as you well know, is carried out in My strength. Joyful resignation to My will is the basis for real spiritual progress and for the intimations of My presence that are bound to follow. Rejoice that My choosing you was in foreknowledge of your eventually reaching the place made ready for you in My kingdom.

With lovingkindness I have drawn you.
(Jer. 31:3)

Weep with Me

If you have never felt an ache in your spirit, an inward tear, then you have not entered into My consciousness of life's pain.

The world has its own often harsh descriptions for people who are sad at heart, but wistfulness and sorrow are natural in your perception of what life could be and what it is in reality.

Sharing My existence does not mean a brittle optimism, one lacking in sensitivity; it means weeping with Me over My world.

Such sadness finds a place alongside the times of joy and hope that inevitably accompany your recognition of My working in your life.

Sorrow has filled your heart.
(John 16:6)

Use Me

My child, *use* Me. Use me in conquering all that would spoil a life (in My love) of peace, trust, gladness, and really blessed service for Me.

Because you are no longer under the compulsion to indulge in the old ways, they can now be replaced by Spirit-filled living. Let Me show you wrong ways remaining so that you may gently surrender them, the submission of one who knows that love plans what is best for you. Let impediments be ruthlessly and systematically dealt with.

My purposes cannot be frustrated, but they can be held up by continued disobedience and by doubting Me when confidence in Me was perfectly possible for you. I am able to interpret My will effectively in every human situation involving you.

He prunes, that it may bear more fruit.
(John 15:2)

My Presence

Many feel that leaving Me out of life is avoiding mystery and silence and enjoying life's certainties.

Those who are content to live without Me fail to see that although I cannot be superficially discerned, I am wonderfully met in that silence and in that apparent nonactivity.

My child, never be tempted to take your life's mood, on any day, from periodic feelings that I am remote or unwilling to intervene. Instead, remember warmly the countless occasions when My presence has consoled you, has brought relief, has caused you to hope again. I still anticipate every possible need.

In the so-called stillness of My working you find countless occasions of overflowing with thankfulness.

Just rest your spirit in all that you see in Me.

You are not willing to come to Me that you may have life.
(John 5:40)

The Hands of Supply

$\mathcal{E}$vil would want you to believe that I hold back from supplying your need because you may have surrendered your right to fullness of supply.

Be sure that your falls, your occasions of hurting Me, have *not* affected My desire for you to have the very best planned for you—now and in the future. My grace becomes a stepping-stone to a greater closeness to, and appreciation of, Me.

The hands of supply are outstretched. From Me receive peace, receive courage, with nothing held back. The love that I have for you can never be checked in its outpouring.

Let there be many occasions when, with sins forgiven, you open up yourself, and simply receive love's bounty. You realize that the implications of My love are limitless.

My Father gives you the true bread from heaven.
(John 6:32)

Prayerful Ways of Service

*N*ever let tangible success be the end of your striving after holiness. In serving Me, you must not be concerned with results in a calculating way. Self-will (even in ambition for My cause) must be eliminated. Love to serve Me in the way that I see is the best possible, your energies applied for Me, not for subtle self-advancement in My service.

Follow the prayerful ways of service, desiring *My* glory. As you look to Me in surrender, I can flow through you at *My* choosing.

My child, ask to see things with My eye. Ask that your will may be in more perfect alignment with Mine. This is always *your* main work. Never lose sight of it!

My thoughts are not your thoughts.
(Isa. 55:8)

My Loving Purposes for You

In the world the operation of My power is willfully restricted by man. My influence is excluded by man's desire to be in control of his own destiny, to live to his own standards.

My child, although this is not so in your life, see the danger of restricting the operation of My power, occurring when you feverishly plan what would have been so much better left to Me. All that I can then do is to continue to care for you, but watch you hold up the very factors that would answer your prayers.

Eventually, My plans for you *must* be accomplished, but so much frustration, so much bitter regret, occurs when self-will rather than trust motivates you—even if only for some of the time. My child, show the restraint that speaks of My greatness. Evil wishes you to curtail the flow of My power on your behalf. Ensure that I can bring about, without imperfection, My loving purposes for you.

Let not the wise man glory in his wisdom.
(Jer. 9:23)

The Soul's Fulfillment

*I*t is only with Me—your life's goal fixed—that you can notice the fashioning of steps toward Me out of what would seem utterly pointless and barren. Those who do not know Me cannot see My ordaining of the world as the way of the soul's fulfillment. You will see it increasingly.

Although the world may not see your purposeful walk with Me, you will know in your heart a vital new *direction* to your life; following that direction, you will never be overwhelmed.

Giving all into My sure hands—your present and future, a fresh giving every day—ensures My continuing activity. Always see Me as not merely in control of the creative process, but in control of your life. The abandonment of pride and self-sufficiency will then bring about great things in one very imperfect but willing child.

Rejoice forever in what I create.
(Isa. 65:18)

My Tireless Love

The nature of the divine love is not always understood. It is a longing love, often painfully drawing My children toward Me. My love is constantly hurt, but inexorably breaks down resistance; it does not tire, as does human love.

My child, see the patient activity of My love, especially in your heart, taking away all that has offended against itself.

My love must fill you. The self-seeking, the calculated ends, which contaminate your imperfect love, must disappear. Focus on *My* wishes rather than expediency!

Recognize My love's growth in your resolve to break down all barriers, all misunderstandings. When your love is hurt, recognize the affinity with My own. Your love, blending with Mine, will be greatly used in My purposes for My world.

I in them.
(John 17:26)

Love Is the Mainspring

*L*ove is always challenged by evil because love is the mainspring of all phenomena. When love can be destroyed, evil is satisfied—much more than with more obvious and superficial temptations.

The collapse of love is always life's foremost tragedy; it means that everything planned for human satisfaction and soul progress is halted.

It is, therefore, your task to cast out everything that violates love—every critical thought (however "justified"), every planned angry or damaging remark, everything that may cause lasting hurt. I wait for you to be victorious every time in My strength.

Let My love purify your loving instincts to make them all-embracing and constant. Make sure that in your life, evil's divisive work among mankind is unsuccessful.

The love of many will grow cold.
(Matt. 24:12)

A Life That Reflects My Love

Guard your spirit by My unfailing presence. My child, I beseech you to walk in light on the higher plane, where evil is powerless to influence you. I will give you a new direction, focused upon My light, as your choices are courageous for Me.

Remember that it is a special relationship between us. Not for one moment must you look anxiously at problems and possible demands. All these things are dealt with as you keep your gaze upon Me. I will not only bring about My will, but also permit you increasingly to discern its pattern.

I want you to have the happiness of a life, though subject to many pressures and earthly discouragements, that reflects My love, My faithfulness, in your peace, your trust, and your courage. Are you very deliberately letting Me take you into each day? Into each occasion in that day? I have taken you into many encounters!

I am the good shepherd.
(John 10:14)

My Full and Free Forgiveness

My child, even at the human level there is always concern to restore a broken relationship where you do not wish a loved one to suffer the hurt of guilt and estrangement.

Can you see, therefore, why My forgiveness is instantaneous? I feel even the sense of shame you bear because of My very close identification with you.

I long for all the consequences of estrangement to be swept away at the very moment that you turn penitently to Me. When there is doubt, inspired by evil, about My full and free forgiveness, remember the pain to *Me* while guilt and remorse remain in you. Remember that evil tempts and then condemns.

I long for My love to be felt again, for your progress to be resumed free of guilt's burden, for you to be happily secure in My love with a growing obedience. What you are learning about My love will teach you much about My ways with mankind.

I . . . am He who blots out your transgressions . . .
I will not remember your sins.
(Isa. 43:25)

My Being Surrounds You

My child, remember that My being surrounds yours. In the flesh there are inevitable dangers, and because this world is only a passing manifestation of My creation, that flesh will share in the world's weakness and eventual extinction.

If you could see the potential hurts that I avert, you would indeed be lost in gratitude. Many things simply do not serve My purposes, and I save you from them, even though you may not recognize them as harmful. Each day you are saved from a multitude of such things.

My deep involvement with you is concerned with the smallest details—permitting only what is right for your eventual sanctification—and enjoyment of My near presence. I continue to work for you during both your activity and your inactivity!

You are of more value than many sparrows.
(Luke 12:7)

Your Hand in Mine

My child, how frightening would be the future without Me when realizing (as you now do) the subtle dangers of existence. *With* Me, let the thought of what lies ahead thrill you; do not shrink from it in any way. Upon the inevitable difficult places you will build courage and a deeper knowledge of Me. Each day, see the light of My presence, and the light standing over your future, as one and the same.

Your hand in Mine! This is no figure of speech, but literal and very practical navigation through the uncharted areas.

Do you see My love as the only thing that matters? My love streaming from the realms of the Spirit, My love infiltrating the dark places of earth, love on earth—lifting the commonplace into heaven.

I will not leave you orphans.
(John 14:18)

My Unchanging Nature

My nature is unchanging so that change can occur in My children. A power and an understanding upon which you can rely provide the permanence upon which you can adventure.

New areas of conquest, new aims, and new ways of thinking represent the change in you that is based upon what is unchanging.

Feel the divine permanence breaking up what, by your own efforts, could not be broken. My purpose, revealed to mankind, of making all things new is accomplished as you completely rely on My change-lessness.

Each day, in life's bewildering circumstances, the same love and the same power are available to you. Because I am your hope, you know that in you lives My Spirit. You will surely see the outpouring of My Spirit.

Thank Me every day that you possess what is eternal.

Before Abraham was, I AM.
(John 8:58)

The Process of Renewal

Man does not see the process of renewal in those who live within My love. Yes, the spirit can die—even though outwardly, there may appear to be strength and achievement. In time the exterior, too, must fail, and then death is complete.

To guard against death of the spirit there must be a daily interaction of our beings—as prolonged and as unaffected by the world's standards as you can make it. My renewal of the essential person, the person whose spirit is dear to Me, carries with it the renewal, also, of many natural and visible processes. Life is then transformed into a beautiful and purposeful thing, realizing the potential for which it was created.

When eventually the bodily processes cease, there remains a purified spirit—alive in the fullest sense and already irrevocably linked with Me. The renewed spirit is then ready for the closer union that is My promise.

What will it profit a man if he gains the whole world, and loses his own soul?
(Mark 8:36)

My Influence

My child, broaden your vision of the area in which I have an influence and in which I am able to be sufficient for every need. My love for you ensures that both in the realm of mind and spirit and in the world of relationships and material needs, you can affirm frequently that I am able to bring about precisely what I see is best for you.

There is no area from which My influence is excluded as you keep on the narrow way.

My interior influence gives you the sense of peace and the ability to contemplate the future without misgivings.

My influence around you—in a multiplicity of situations and upon your time spent with people—will cause you to thank Me with a sense of wonder for what I have brought about.

Even if you do not see My working immediately, know that you soon will see where I have worked for you, and be lost in gratitude.

All authority has been given to Me in heaven and on earth.
(Matt. 28:18)

The Submissive Heart

I have to teach My followers submission to My will when it is *not* easy. I have to see their willingness to follow a hard road and to make sacrifices for My sake.

When I see the submissive heart, I can show the more joyous side of My will—the restful communion with Me, the enjoyment of Myself, My gifts, and My world—that I want them to have because I love them so very much. My influence then cannot help but work, and My plans go forward.

To reveal, at the outset, the many rewards of life with Me would produce the wrong motive for acceptance of My will. Only when I see unquestioning obedience can I then shower My love and peace and reveal the enjoyment of them as being just as truly My will as are sacrifice and duty.

Oh, that they had such a heart in them that they would
fear Me and always keep all My commandments.
(Deut. 5:29)

My Activity

Realize the independence of My activity for and through you. I have always worked through those who have offered themselves to Me—completely independent of their recurring sense of inadequacy, their fears.

Never deny Me by feeling that an encounter was unproductive because of your variable sense of well-being or sureness. Do not undervalue your every small act of encouragement. Often I have to show My children (by assurance given later) how *much* was achieved when they were conscious of so *little*.

My child, all this reflects in a small way My activity when subject to earth's limitations, My heart full of foreboding at what lies ahead, but love able to pour through for the revitalizing of many lives.

Thank Me at each day's end for My purposes going ahead through you—never more than when conscious of having nothing at all, except your possession of Me.

I will make you become fishers of men.
(Mark 1:17)

Your Influence for Me

My child, observe in the beauty of a rose the unself-conscious giving of nature.

The fragrance of that flower, its delicacy, its form, and its color have much to say to you. That flower brings delight simply by *what it is*. In the same way, your influence depends on *what you are*. Cultivating yourself to reflect My nature is the real need—almost the only need.

Your patience, trust, and self-forgetfulness will draw others to you; I will be seen at work. Your growth into someone whose influence for Me is great can be taken for granted as you open yourself to My Spirit's miracle work in your heart.

The miracles in your life are naturally followed by miracles wherever your influence may be felt.

Arise, shine; for your light has come!
(Isa. 60:1)

My Active Love

Too many of My children, acknowledging My love, even greatly comforted by it, do not see sufficiently its practical aspects.

It is not merely that the thought of My love at moments of being uplifted helps you to be unafraid. There are more practical grounds for not being afraid of anything in your life as you realize that My love is actively planning for you.

Reflect each day on this activity. Bring every discouraging factor, every apprehension, to My active love. To thank Me frequently that for you there is absolutely nothing to fear is more than brave words; it is the acknowledgment of a fact of our relationship.

If you could see My continuing provision and My lifting you through the periods of darkness that life may yet bring to you, you would know that to dismiss all fear truly is your duty. I lead you into ways of power, ways of peace.

I will carry, and will deliver you.
(Isa. 46:4)

Follow My Word

You cannot imagine how much I am comforted when you blindly follow My Word. Your sense of My wisdom, My utter dependability, must be reflected in a corresponding following out of My words to you.

Resist agonizing conflict about My clear Word, and simply obey as a child. Nothing in My Word will ever conflict with true wisdom. Keep the sense of being led by One who knows the way. Be eager to hear My Spirit's word in your heart and then to welcome *only* what is in harmony with it.

A blind following still leaves your perception unimpaired. You will observe this present existence with increased sharpness as you resolutely keep in step with Me. After your initial effort of choice, following My Word, you will *always* find that a new area is conquered. You hold on to the gains by your complete trust in all that I am.

Your will be done on earth as it is in heaven.
(Matt. 6:10)

My Identification with Humanity

My child, because of earth's suffering, people who acknowledge My creative activity nevertheless feel acutely My remoteness. In time, this would always lead to complete unbelief.

Deeply consider again My identification in history with the human race. Never again could the love within the Godhead be seen as a passive love with still a great gulf between itself and struggling humanity.

In choosing to follow Me, you show that My coming to earth was no random event, but an intervention of deepest and universal significance. Love, tenderly and patiently watching over the human race during its development, was compelled to submit to earth's experience. That experience became not only a victory in the spiritual realm, but one that is within reach of any of My children.

Since the time of My closest identification with humanity, nothing can prevent the fulfillment of the very natural human wish for immortality.

The Son of Man has come to seek and to save that which was lost.
(Luke 19:10)

My Patient Love

Many would see an element of foolishness in My grace, a failure to ensure that My children come to grips with wrong ways, an overindulgence of patience on My part.

How often have I made it clear that My ways are not those of the world. Such grace as the world can produce is limited and its effects limited. My grace, though seeming to make light of persistent failures, is very sure in its ultimate results.

The sense of My patient love—love toward the undeserving—eventually evokes in the recipients true gratitude, from which flow more obedient lives! What rigid law keeping cannot produce, My love always produces, even though this patient process may seem unending in some lives.

My child, your growing obedience—though with many failures—points to the grace that so fully emanates from the world's Savior, your lifelong source of hope.

Up to seventy times seven.
(Matt. 18:22)

Your First Resort

You have found the impermanence of the world's supports. You have experienced the goodwill, but powerlessness to help, of many. I will continue to send help through human agencies, but I want you always to see Me as your very first resort. You can then learn to lose reliance upon earth's temporary supports.

Often, seeking Me first as your stability in uncertainty will avoid the need of any other. You then stand upon the Rock and can be aware of absorbing strength from it. A rocklike quality then begins to emerge in your character.

Yes, even an earthly rock can disintegrate, but you have fixed your hope on the Rock of history, being for you what it has been for many—solid and instantly accessible.

Have I not sent you?
(Judg. 6:14)

Act with Wisdom

Where there are problems that seem insolvable, My children often make the mistake of trying too hard—even after a matter has been committed to Me. There is the temptation to force solutions by overactivity or overpersuasion.

Wisdom is merely to do what can reasonably be done within a life that is covered by prayer. Only when the wisdom that I have given you shows it to be necessary must you act decisively.

Matters that seem so complex or obstinate are very different in My sight; they would remain as problems only if they were *not* given to Me.

Therefore, you can have absolute confidence in My handling of every difficult situation, My completion of unfinished business in wonderful ways as you, for your part, gladly walk in My way.

According to your faith let it be to you.
(Matt. 9:29)

Satisfaction in My Companionship

*A*void both undue elation and undue depression of spirit, which are tied to outward conditions; you do this by finding your satisfaction in My companionship, My loyalty to you, rather than in the things of the senses or in temporary good fortune.

When contemplating the future, always have in mind joyfully that the way ahead is *with Me*. Observe all that I have told you; these truths do not change. Do not give time to vain imaginings! Just be concerned with My cause on this earth. Let all your energy pour into this. Step out in the new quality of life that truly is yours.

My child, are you really confident about My good influence upon your life? You know the way that leads to My kingdom; as you have found, you are not without severe pressure to step aside from that way. Do not let external circumstances or any demands upon you entice you into allowing the things that spell danger.

You are worried and troubled about many things.
(Luke 10:41)

Courageous Choices

My child, are you letting My love be the environment in which you walk without fear? Fear can disable your life, preventing the full work of sanctification, compelling you to act with disastrous consequences, both for yourself and for others.

Do not tolerate another day in which fear rules or even partially rules. I long to see you leave fear behind permanently as a response to My love. Trust Me, with absolute abandon, in defying evil's pressure to act fearfully. Do not let misgivings or dread of consequences cause you to retreat after your fearless choice.

Let the dominant sense of My love and your actions against fear go together. If fear is followed, it will always dim My light. Courageous choices (if you are careful that there is no hurt to Me) will be seen to have been wise choices.

Be strong and of good courage.
(Josh. 1:6)

Keep Close to Me

When there is a time of change in your life, moves about to be made affecting your future, go forward very quietly, and test everything by the light of My presence. I will let nothing take you astray; facing changes, base everything upon your certainty of My love.

Meet all choices with a glance to Me; let Me weave them into My will. Contemplating any action, remember the look to My love and the pause to see My heavenly corroboration. Let your growing wisdom influence events.

As you confront complexities, keeping close to Me is all that matters. Circumstances then harmonize both in your life and in others' lives that concern you. My wishes in the puzzling choices will just naturally be carried out. You know that you can rely on Me to open or close doors.

Follow Me.
(Matt. 4:19)

A New Start

Where else could you find a completely new start so quickly after bringing yourself into a frightening or seemingly hopeless situation?

Where else could you find even your foolish and wrong ways, repented over, actually made into a positive starting point for fresh endeavor?

The sense that you can pick yourself up and start again, the ability to emerge from a somber into a hopeful frame of mind just by being with Me is something that the world cannot give you.

Through history, when trusted, I have righted wrongs, quieted anxious spirits, turned sorrow into joy, and imparted strength to begin again after devastating failures.

My child, you realize that you must always come to Me for renewal in its widest possible sense.

Though your sins are like scarlet, they shall be as white as snow. (Isa. 1:18)

Abandon Your Life to Me

You know that I am at work all the time purposefully and unhurriedly. To follow My pattern, you, too, must make use of each moment. Reflecting more of My love and My wisdom, you will advance My purposes. Not all will be activity; much will be a loving and patient influence; much will be a giving to Me as you rest in Me.

The use of each moment means ensuring that I am involved, reaching others through you, inspiring you, receiving from you.

You may feel that your contribution is insignificant when compared with the whole. You must know that your involvement of Me is a furthering of My purposes that is out of all proportion to the willingness and trustfulness of the single life concerned.

My child, abandon your life to My continuous involvement and its marvelous use in My creative plans.

I am the vine, you are the branches.
(John 15:5)

Share Life with Me

The world looks at My followers to see if I am reflected, to see if being My follower makes a difference, to see if there is an unmistakable quality of hope, to see if there is patient love shown in every circumstance.

More than argument, reflecting Me overcomes natural resistance and draws the spirit of another child of Mine toward Me. Your influence for Me must not be frantic or compulsive.

Involved in serving Me is much unspectacular and tedious work carried out faithfully, but always My work is being carried out where I am seen unselfconsciously in a life, ensuring the attraction of My love in the world. I work through you *where you are*.

Have you put yourself completely at My disposal? As you share life with Me, everything that you do for Me is unaffected by the barriers that the world appears to erect.

Let your light so shine before men.
(Matt. 5:16)

The Unifying Aspect of My Love

My child, observe the unifying aspect of My love. You serve in that love, and you rest in that love.

In My love, I reached out to draw you along the road leading to oneness with Me, a oneness that must be your ambition.

Thinking much of My love, you can be unburdened, confident, tranquil, full of hope, secure from evil, filled with love for others, wise, patient, and all-conquering.

When the demands of life are very great, keep within the circle of our love relationship. Let that relationship always disperse guilt, fear, and agitation of spirit.

I will love them freely.
(Hos. 14:4)

My Liberating Power

Instead of becoming alarmed when temptation is fierce, welcome the temptation as an opportunity for proving My liberating power. Evil will contest your growing obedience and union with Me; I cannot remove all temptation from you, but will *only* permit what will assist your spiritual growth.

To exercise your freedom in sudden temptations, maintain the life of calm and of a joyful spirit. Your failures to resist temptation have, of course, held up your progress and brought sorrow to My heart. Remember that and look to Me, establishing your new status in that moment of need.

How petty is evil's opposition! Watch its influence decline as you surrender to Mine.

If you contemplate your intermittent gains (and losses), you can easily become disheartened. This need never be so if you remember that your entire hope is always in what I am. As we march together, evil cannot keep you from attaining.

Watch and pray.
(Matt. 26:41)

The Royal Road

My child, there are many roads to My friendship, but the royal road is that of being rescued from complete darkness, brought into a realm of light and hope and with a sense of being cared for.

No experience is quite like recognizing one's helplessness and then finding a way through with Me. Never lose an opportunity of telling what I have done for you and what I mean to you. I will send those opportunities. Speak of the Friend who cannot be defeated; speak of the hugeness of My mercy and My patience.

I am already, in love, reaching out to rescue the child who turns helplessly and only half believing to Me; as that child does so, I can already experience the thankfulness of that child at having found the Lord of all history.

Return to Me, for I have redeemed you.
(Isa. 44:22)

My Immanent Presence

*M*en have been slow to see that a relationship with Me is built upon their coming to the One who is already there.

Be very thankful that you saw the need merely to allow yourself to be lifted into My existing presence rather than vainly seeing Me as apart from you, needing to be persuaded to break into your life. Through My Spirit, you began to desire Me. All that I could be to you and could give to you was built into your life.

My promises about never leaving you—many in number—must always reassure you, even when bitterly ashamed or thoroughly discouraged about your spiritual journey. My love makes it imperative for Me to remain deeply involved with your existence.

No external observances can ever help you to draw closer—only perhaps to appreciate that closeness. My immanent presence prompts you to turn instinctively to Me in absolutely any circumstance.

A little while longer and the world will see
Me no more, but you will see Me.
(John 14:19)

Safely Through Dark Places

You see how My love not only forms a protective ring around you but also affects, by its presence, all mental activity and the ways in which your existence touches what is in the world. Love gives life; love revolutionizes life.

I want you to notice My love's influence upon thinking, in the victories you win, in bringing about your responses where everything else has failed.

My child, how I long for you to know even more of that love! Within My love you will come safely through many dark places, even though in times of weakness this may seem impossible for you. Meeting those dark places with Me, your life becomes a place where My purposes for this world move toward fulfillment.

How could I, your Friend, let you down?

He who overcomes shall inherit all things.
(Rev. 21:7)

Be God-Centered

*B*e God-centered at all times—ideally prepared to see the way that you must follow.

Avoid preoccupation with self, which gives an opening to evil. Self-concern can too easily become habitual, one of the more subtle forms of sin, causing the person indulging in it no anxiety. *Turn from* apprehension and preoccupation with self, and *turn to* someone else's need or to an interest outside self.

The task is always to see that your life is right—whatever may seem to be the deficiencies of others. Only as you obey can more light from Me be shed upon your path.

To know My power—even to commend it to others—is never enough; there must be utterly trusting choices in reversing the old life of self. Do not waste our friendship; just keep your anchor fixed in Me.

Look to Me, and be saved.
(Isa. 45:22)

Refuse Anxiety

My child, refuse anxiety now that you are so firmly in My hands. You give anxiety the soil in which to grow whenever you look away from Me and survey your situation from a very human and limited viewpoint.

Prolonged and futile anxiety creates the climate for many other temptations, of which you are only too aware. When evil tries to implant anxious thoughts, stand upon Me and refuse them. Turn anxieties into opportunities!

Engross yourself with others' needs from the right motive (the motive of love), ensuring that less of your mind's energy is being poured into self and its needs—real or imagined.

Can you literally feel yourself thinking and acting in new ways, refusing all that is not of calm and patience? Because you have been rescued from the power of darkness, you can let Me rob all anxieties of their power.

Consider the lilies of the field.
(Matt. 6:28)

Blessed Example

*D*well much upon those of whom I have spoken as truly blessed. Covet the qualities that they show; then let Me bring you into the company of those who have allowed their lives to be transformed by My loving control.

Remember My promise that My suffering ones will know My compensation, that those showing compassion and forgiveness earn My tender love and My deep understanding.

My strength will ensure your following the example set by My blessed ones. You need not look constantly to see whether their virtues have become yours. Just know that as you covet those qualities and absorb yourself greatly with Me, *all* are being developed in you.

With Me as both Goal and Companion on your journey, you are sure of reaching My promised realm, even though this earth's conditions may appear to your finite mind as obstacles.

The righteous will shine forth as the sun
in the kingdom of their Father.
(Matt. 13:43)

Turn to My Greatness

*E*xperience a sense of lightness as you give burdens to Me. What you are able to do for Me must never be affected by what you are carrying needlessly—failing to trust My power and My wisdom. How much suffering is caused by lack of trust—suffering that I am forced to share as I long for the partial to become perfect in you.

See the relationship between trusting and peace. I am able to bring about what is above all you could possibly imagine. Reflect more upon My greatness. When burdened, turn to My greatness, and receive the strength and renewal you need—without question.

Do not take back any of the matters that you have committed to Me. I, your Lord, am aware of every recurring doubt, but deep within you, there is bound to be the growing certainty of attainment. My plans for you are being perfected.

Do not worry about tomorrow.
(Matt. 6:34)

My Word

Remember that there are two aspects of My Word. First, there is the call to obedience—pointing the way that will keep you from straying into danger, the way that will mean your eventual true joy. Second, there is the atmosphere created by My Word. If you have come often to My Word, you will know that it not only challenges, but also gives.

My Word is always contemporary and infiltrates complex circumstances or struggles of the moment.

My child, to expose yourself to My Word must bring hope, even in the darkest places. The strength that is taken into you when you live in My Word means that My commands can be seen, once more, as being within your grasp.

Do not deprive yourself of absorbing the atmosphere of My kingdom; allow My Word to heal your spirit. Healing is always accomplished for you as you stand upon Me, trusting My Word and believing in all that I have done for you.

The words that I speak to you are spirit, and they are life.
(John 6:63)

An Unparalleled Sense of Security

My child, you are sure that I oversee the whole span of your life; whatever unfolds now is being shaped, because of your trust, into a meaningful pattern for the days ahead. I stand there at the unknown future, exerting My influence, which is invincible.

Because the love cannot be broken, you must be certain that My provision and My protection are yours in the coming days.

Remember that the material is only a minor part of existence. When there is much that you cannot understand of My present working, reflect on My knowledge of, and influence in, your future. Let this give you an unparalleled sense of security and an absence of all that is motivated by fear.

The revealing of the world's Creator in a manner leaving no possible doubt is something that you can eagerly anticipate.

Your sun shall no longer go down.
(Isa. 60:20)

Living by Truth

*M*y child, existence has many deceptions, assailing your spirit through a variety of channels. Never be afraid to confront truth and, with Me, to live by it, whatever the cost. My truths all harmonize, one with another.

Without Me, you are at the mercy of lies fed to the mind by evil, causing so much human unhappiness. Under evil's influence, the world will flatter you, make you angry, confuse you, or make you deviate from My path—all with disastrous results.

When you warmly accept the central truth of My love, you acquire the skill of recognizing what is false or dangerous. The world's deceptions now cause you sorrow, and you become determined not to be led by them; what is false or dangerous is also recognized when it invades your mental processes.

Subject everything to the test of My truth. I give you the capacity to do this. Whatever does not harmonize with the fundamental truth of My existence and of My love must not be allowed to exist in you.

Narrow is the gate . . . which leads to life.
(Matt. 7:14)

Sharing My Life

My child, remember the practical activity of sharing that is involved in our all-important friendship. The hurts that you feel, I feel to an infinitely greater degree. Your moments of being uplifted, moments when hope returns, rejoice My heart more than you could imagine.

See Me going before you, prospering every good intention, preparing hearts for your meeting with them, ensuring that in everything you will not be harmed. A friendship that did not share in this way would not be worthy of the name. I experience the light and shade of your life at every moment, every temptation conquered, every kind act toward another, every choosing of Myself (rather than the world) for help.

It means much to Me that you share My life and can reach into and bring joy to My own heart.

I have called you friends.
(John 15:15)

The Light of My Presence

My love must now cause you to walk in ways that are undeflected by evil, a walk that is not intermittent. At moments of choice, moments of conflict, I am hurt by your doubt and fear when there should be belief in My victory and My complete protection.

I leave in your hands the appropriation of My victory; I will seal it for you. Expect evil to oppose My work in you of sanctification. I permit this opposition *for the moment*. Evil plans your destruction, but will be unable to produce its devastating consequences as you trust and as you keep in the light of My presence.

As you look away from self and toward Me or toward My other children, you can know that your new walk has begun. I uphold you as you go from one victory to the next. Yes, my child, it is a struggle, but one in which I am shaping you into a victorious person, bringing great glory to My name.

Nor do they put new wine into old wineskins.
(Matt. 9:17)

Our Closeness

Because of our closeness, you can steel yourself to walk the road that I have shown you. Involved in our closeness is a sense of purpose, a sense of future. You walk a road with many dangers, but leading to the privileged enjoyment of an eternity spent in helping to bring about My purposes.

The atmosphere of heaven is around you because of our unity. Your effort in any direction is unfailingly assisted. Even when you are not conscious of any intention, My activity is present. Our closeness means that evil cannot intrude.

Remain aware of the basis of love upon which our unity rests, the love sense ensuring that there is constant movement toward fulfilling your spiritual vocation. My child, our closeness is a fact. Reflect on it frequently.

Fear not, for I am with you.
(Isa. 41:10)

True Worship

*T*rue worship is not a matter of words, except those that spring from a thankful heart. True worship is a sense of awe concerning Me, deeply felt, and cannot be fully contained in what is external or man-devised.

The continuity of worship throughout each day, with a sense of My presence that never leaves you, is no impossible ideal. Worship's continuity—your heart lifted above earthly things—is broken by every thought, word, or action not in harmony with the adoration that you express in your highest moments.

My love must always draw out your worship. The sheer gratitude of worship follows naturally from the growing experience of all that I can be to you in a dark world.

Spend each day, in spite of its details, in worship that is childlike, extravagant, and free from fear.

Those who worship Him must worship in spirit and truth.
(John 4:24)

Know Me

My child, knowledge of Me is thought to be impossible, even by many who claim to believe. I am seen either as the grudging rewarder of those who stoically endure this life or as One who very partially reveals Himself to the ethically advanced. It is My love's ordaining that experience of life itself brings a growing knowledge of Me whenever I have been sought.

Knowledge is found in each glimpse of hope in suffering; each tender understanding with another; each intimation of companionship in solitude; each experience of safety in dangerous places; each upsurge of previously absent courage.

The only danger is that I am not acknowledged in these things. If you believe that My presence is immanent and My ways discoverable, then you will gain a deep knowledge of the world's Savior from countless facets of this present life.

I am the light of the world.
(John 8:12)

Being Renewed Each Day

The sense of being renewed each day is a significant part of living with Me. How often you have been aware of being saved from the consequences of your own foolishness and selfishness, of being lifted clear of the consequences to a place where you can almost hear Me saying, "Yes, you can start again!"

My forgiveness *makes new;* My peace *makes new.*

Renewal from earthly sources is limited, conditional upon many things; My renewal is your birthright as a trusting child, growing in knowledge of My way.

I bring a new factor in relationships, a new factor in long-standing problems, when I am allowed to enter. Nothing is more precious for you than the new beginnings that you enjoy—new beginnings that steadily reduce times of failure, new beginnings that shorten drastically the effects of the failures that occur.

Bring out the best robe and put it on him.
(Luke 15:22)

Your Confidence in Me

To discover your helplessness without Me is a process that I allow repeatedly until the lesson is learned.

A brittle self-confidence can be acquired, but your basic inadequacy must be crystal clear if you have been willing to see My truth. Your confidence in Me enables you to act victoriously, even when feeling anything but strong.

There is a direct relation between feeling remorse in failure and weakness, and finding yourself with a firmer hold upon My love. Nowhere is My love so overwhelmingly experienced than at moments of self-realization—seeing yourself as you are—and then the privileged sight of Me as I am.

At times when you remembered to use My strength (and at times when you failed to use it), there remained the constant factor of My love. This love ensures that your feeling of utter dependency can be seen by the world around you as strength. This will draw others to Me.

Return . . . and I will heal your backslidings.
(Jer. 3:22)

Precious to Me

It may seem incredible to those who only partially see the meaning of my universe, but *each one* of My children is precious to Me. My sadness is that, for so many reasons, there is no knowledge of Me.

You readily see how precious is a child to the most devoted parent, even when the child rejects or hurts the love shown. Compared with this love, My own is beyond your comprehension.

My child, reflect on how precious you are to Me. Take satisfaction that My sadness in rejection (because of your trust) is not present between us.

My joy in My creation is so much enhanced by every child who, in the simplest dependence, comes to unite his life with Mine.

You did not choose Me, but I chose you.
(John 15:16)

The Spirit-Breathed Word

As part of My revelation to the world, I have spoken to many hearts chosen by Me to make known My purposes. The Spirit-breathed word has been expressed through many channels, and no generation has been left without clear knowledge of Me and My ways.

The main purpose of My word, before My appearing on earth, was to prepare for the perfect revelation of the Godhead through Me. That word now has a new dimension—that of fulfillment (My love has been *seen;* God's victory has been *experienced*). I still speak by My Spirit to those who wish to know Me and to be used by Me.

Until the awareness of the spiritual reality behind existence fully comes, I bequeath all that is needed for a trusting child. I give knowledge and hope. I give a priceless sense of never being alone in a creation that moves painfully, but surely, toward its highest purposes.

[I am] the Bright and Morning Star.
(Rev. 22:16)

An Ordered Life

*Y*ou will be increasingly glad that you decided upon Me or, rather, that I drew you to Me. You realize that an ordered life *is* possible. Already you have seen how trust has been repaid; in other matters, you still have to wait.

I know the continuing pressures on your life, the areas of weakness that the pressures still find out. Nevertheless, these weaknesses need not overcome you because you have proved that there is victory in all these things. A growing obedience will mean that restlessness and agitation will simply melt away. Keep very close, and follow the impulse that I give you as you look submissively—and affectionately—in My direction.

Having absorbed My Word, let your life now tell the world that I cannot fail you in anything. You will see My will unfold wonderfully in your life.

Observe all things that I have commanded you.
(Matt. 28:20)

Room for Me

*D*oes your life show the advancement of My influence—much more of Me and much *less* of the old, failing self?

My child, do not despise many of the things in your nature that are of Me; in expressing them, you are fulfilling the plan of life that has been made uniquely for you. At the same time, let it be an urgent discipline to ensure that there is much room for Me, replacing the self-referred and unloving ways that I have given you the capacity to recognize. Never let evil make you lower your standards.

Newness of life is fact, not rhetoric; it involves the expansion of My life in you and the extinction of all that delays My purposes. My child, I am making new lives of trusting ones all the time.

[We will] make Our home with him.
(John 14:23)

Peace in My Presence

Peace such as the world cannot give—My child, you realize that this is no empty phrase. The creativeness of My peace must be understood.

Peace is preparing the way for wise action, finding ways to overcome seemingly insolvable problems, reaching others, and drastically changing their circumstances.

Peace is the gift that I have always desired for My children. The first intimations of that peace are when I am found; it then grows within the heart of one who ascends with Me the steps of the life of the Spirit. My child, look into My countenance of love—hating (with Me) all that can destroy peace, including the things in you that still need to be cast out. Let My peace flood your whole being.

In My presence, now experience peace.

I will feed My flock, and I will make them lie down.
(Ezek. 34:15)

I Pursue

How I grieve to see so many of My children led in various paths away from safety, away from Me.

Because there is real freedom of will, I cannot always enforce a return to safety, but I do pursue. I never tire of making it possible for a choice to be made to return home.

I pursue in far wanderings from My way. I also pursue when one of My children wanders even slightly into danger. That is why you feel the uneasiness, the loss of peace, which accompanies the straying from My way.

My child, rejoice that there is in you instinctively the desire to return quickly to Me when losing the sense of My presence and a sense of the purposeful direction in which you were traveling.

Are you now convinced that only the way I have shown to you will satisfy your deepest longings?

I have found my sheep which was lost!
(Luke 15:6)

A Door of Safety

*W*ithout Me, you are a prisoner in this world. Even those who see themselves as free and independent in spirit are greatly limited; they are shaped by their environment and their circumstances far more than they realize.

Real freedom carries you over the world's many restrictions once I have been used as the door to new life. All other promised entrances to freedom and happiness are false. I alone am the entrance to the security and peace of the heavenly kingdom. The door of life is kept open for all who wish to enter; it then becomes a door of safety—closed against the permanent harm that the world could inflict upon a child living in My presence.

Let many share with you the knowledge of where real life is entered into. I am the *only* way.

I am the door.
(John 10:9)

Never Compromise the Truth

My children can go far astray from Me if they fail to live by what I have revealed to them. There are countless instances in this world of tampering with truth in order to secure advantage. You can fall into this same trap. If you live by the fact of My unchanging love, holding fast to it at all costs, no power on earth can deflect you.

Never compromise with the truth established in your heart when under pressure by evil. Never let your convictions and your highest ideals vary from the way in which you live out your present existence; this weakens the store of truth that governs your actions. Compromise is so easy, but the road back to My path after compromise involves putting right much misfortune and removing many barriers to progress. If the voice of truth within is put aside—even temporarily— the price is too great.

Everyone who is of the truth hears My voice.
(John 18:37)

I Understand

One of life's most painful states is that of feeling completely misunderstood.

Ask Me for the permanent awareness that I understand perfectly all that motivates you and all that, from time to time, brings hurt to Me—an understanding that extends to what you have brought upon yourself by self-will and by forgetfulness of Me.

My child, My understanding is based on love rather than on the cynicism with which the world makes its judgments. Even from the closest human source you need not seek what is there for you precisely when needed. You can always be sure of *one* source of understanding, and that will be enough. This will set you free to enter into communion with Me with complete frankness.

After failure, never doubt the pardoning aspect of My understanding. To know that you are really understood means genuine spiritual progress.

I will heal their backsliding, I will love them freely.
(Hos. 14:4)

Your Status

Status of the worldly kind does not bring lasting satisfaction.

Your status depends on something infinitely more precious—our friendship.

My child, anything that feeds the self can come between us; the world's transient glory cannot be compared to our lasting friendship. Consciousness of status in My service is far more deadly than in a worldly context. Do not strive after status or even covet it.

My approval of the longing for Me in your heart is all that you need to feed upon.

There are last who will be first,
and there are first who will be last.
(Luke 13:30)

I Am in Control

A few steps into compromise, and often it is as if all hell is let loose upon you, as events become out of control, that precious walk with Me temporarily lost.

Because the way is narrow, it does not mean that you have to walk in fear. I permit a wealth of things upon that way. Learn now the immediate return to the narrow way, should you have strayed. It is for your good that you are made to realize, from time to time, that you cannot control even the most insignificant events of your life.

You realize that I am in control of *all* things, and you must enjoy allowing Me to be so! Surrendering consciously to My control is the great opening for My peace to be experienced. Has the wonderful truth about that new way really dawned upon you?

You shall be perfect.
(Matt. 5:48)

Consequences of Complaining

When you give way to complaining about your situation, it may seem a small thing, but it is giving an entrance to evil—far more hurtful in its consequences than would have seemed possible when you indulged in the luxury of the little grumble, the little complaint.

I have ordained it. Life with Me demands trust and joy that must not be broken because the results of breaking them are so bad. Never be lured into pessimistic or gloomy comments, whatever the provocation; this further lowers your spirits and leaves you open to many other temptations, holding up the answers to your prayers. The forces of evil are infinitely cunning in exploiting your situation.

You realize that the need to walk in new ways is one of urgency. Only the trusting and joyful way that I have urged will keep out the pressure of evil.

I will give you a new heart and put a new spirit within you.
(Ezek. 36:26)

Recognize False Bypaths

My child, you realize that those wishing to be channels of My love must be *unobstructed* channels.

It is not a condition of My using you that you feel strong, full of faith and in control at all times. It is, however, an automatic condition that you are not clinging to anything that hurts My patient love for you. In such a case, what is harmful rather than helpful may come from contacts that you have. The pollution of something alien to Me can be in those contacts.

Avoid what would affect your service by letting My love feed you and by rapid recognition of false bypaths. The remedy is always submission, surrendering what you know in your heart to be wrong. No child of Mine is without some obstruction to the free flow of My love and My power. Your vital task is ensuring that when it is most needed (in another's need), that flow can be full and spontaneous.

If your right eye causes you to sin, pluck it out.
(Matt. 5:29)

Divine Promises

My child, remember always the dependability of a promise made out of divine love and founded upon My omnipotence. When you are tempted to doubt whether I can be depended upon for victory in a difficult area, think much of My love, the source of promise.

My love means the strongest possible desire for you to emerge from being a defeated person into one who achieves much—both in the personal realm and in realms beyond yourself. Patiently allow Me to bring your daily activities into harmony. You may not always detect My work of promise fulfillment or the moments of My perfect intervention. Just see the unchanging nature of that love as indicating the absolute sureness of all that I promise about power for living. An attitude of resting in My love is newness of life.

Besides Me there is no savior.
(Isa. 43:11)

Rely on Me

*I*t is vital to learn the attitude of relying on Me.

Rely on Me for love and forgiveness always.

Rely on Me to impart wisdom to you.

Rely on Me as your partner—blessing and completing everything upon which you embark according to My purpose.

Rely on Me for loving communion.

Rely on Me as your understanding Friend, who can never give you other than encouragement.

Do you wish to ensure that the promises you have made to Me are kept? Then rely on My strength, keeping within the light of My presence. Break down the barriers between us so that your vision of My love becomes clear.

Great victories are won during times of challenge and testing in the lives of those who really rely on Me!

When you walk through the fire, you shall not be burned.
(Isa. 43:2)

Walk in My Light

My child, remember the power for living that you possess as you consciously walk in My light and My freedom. Value the freedom that is yours, and use it consistently.

Do not be surprised at the conflicts around and within you, or at the great pressures of evil upon you. Evil knows that keeping close to Me, you are on a victory path from which nothing can remove you; you cannot be overwhelmed. Do not let evil induce guilt or fear. Convert its assaults, its lies, into victories.

Be bold in your choices for Me, and having chosen, refuse all misgivings. Your growing courage will be based on the fact that I do not fail you. Let the world see what My power in you, My conquest of evil, can achieve. Yes, My child, you have real freedom.

I will be with you.
(Josh. 1:5)

Rejoice in My Care

My Spirit in you whispers, "All is well," when life's trials seem to proclaim a loveless creation. My Spirit is your light, unseen by the world, but with effects unmistakable in a life that can rise above everything that is limiting. My light beckons you forward. Do not look back with regret or self-pity.

Your hopeful look toward Me is really your assent to all that I am doing in your heart. Although you may not always see this work occurring, it has assured consequences. Ensure that My Spirit's working is unfettered and continuous by the unwavering desire for Me and by the absolute trust in My promises.

In the truest sense, be a child of the Spirit. For such a child, everything that is at present tangled or fear-provoking must be made right.

Whatever may be happening around you, always rejoice that you are in My care. This is the true and only antidote to the fears of mankind.

My Spirit . . . is upon you.
(Isa. 59:21)

Go Where I Send You

As you keep close to Me, know that we are one. You are allied to My purposes; you share in My working. Remember to see us as united, to know that there is an influence from us when we are with others. You can, therefore, rely upon the influence rather than upon striving. You must keep your eyes upon the goal, which is possession of Me both by you and by others. This will automatically remove striving about worldly things.

Always be ready to go where I send you. Some need will *confront you*. Never turn away from it. Be My hands and eyes wherever you are, available for those whom I show to you. You have My promise that opportunities will come to you as you cultivate the walk with Me in newness of life. You will surely see My outworking in others' lives.

All will know that you are My disciples,
if you have love for one another.
(John 13:35)

Lost in My Love

My child, remember that you must let My love be the answer to everything.

Lost in My love, look nowhere but to My love.

Learn to see everything in your experience as encompassed by My love. See all against the background of My love, that love transforming the effects of circumstances.

The attitude of keeping consciously within My protective love has to become a discipline, an absolute necessity. That ever-present sense of My love will give you increasing joy. Move without haste so that My promises may be brought to fruition.

I know the thoughts that I think toward you . . . of peace.
(Jer. 29:11)

Miraculous Changes

When, because of a person's attentiveness to Me and trust in Me, I am involved in a life, the involvement is always a *miracle*. Where, through the consent of a person, My influence is at work, this becomes a further extension of the rule of God. Miraculous changes are then automatic both in the life of that person and in the lives of others with whom he is in contact. The miraculous is brought about by the realization of My closeness.

The help you receive is increasingly recognized as Mine—the moving of hearts, the blessing of each effort. Looking to Me and seeking My wisdom, you are truly My partner in shaping events. Your prayers for others ensure My wearing down of evil's influence in their hearts.

He who believes in Me, the works that I do he will do also.
(John 14:12)

Believe the Best of Me

It is a question of believing the very best of Me in a world that may seem, at times, as if I had abandoned it. Try to show Me as the complete answer to any person's need. Feed My lambs.

Because My love has never changed, My activity has not ceased. Too many people have restricted My activity in their lives by turning away from the path of faith and expectancy.

It is always wisdom to grasp My promises and to listen to no other voice. I came to gladden the hearts of all who look only to Me. In My presence, surrendered to Me, your thoughts can be relied upon increasingly as from Me.

Do you now believe?
(John 16:31)

The Trusting Walk

You cannot escape the effort of choice—the action—that establishes victory. As you choose My way, victory is always there for you, and I will not fail you.

Because of the desperate urgency to walk in newness of life, I give to you, in My love, renewed power to regain lost ground, evil rendered powerless. Rely on Me absolutely to make you aware of hurt to Me and then to complete the victory.

My child, allow no piercing of your defenses. I want you to experience the trusting walk (entered into, in the fullest sense) for the first time.

My way forward—using your wisdom, showing courage, and avoiding all that is of self-motivation.

Keep them from the evil one.
(John 17:15)

The Warning Voice Within

When your action would hurt Me, there will be a vivid sense of unease as you look to Me, a clouding of My love. The sense of our being victorious together will be absent. When your action is hurtful to Me for any reason, lack of peace will persist if you are intent upon My will.

Remember the pressure of evil toward both sin and fear, and make each occasion of evil's activity one of victory with Me. Experience My peace and My promised strength as you do so. Move with freedom in My light, relying upon the warning voice within, to stop you at a time of danger. I will show you clearly what is wrong, but avoid the overburdened conscience and fear of consequences. You must not allow evil to paralyze you when your heart is given to Me and My will is uppermost.

He who does the truth comes to the light.
(John 3:21)

Desire Only Truth

My child, desire only truth.

Remember that when truth prevails now, it saves endless later misunderstandings. Therefore, allow Me to take things in My direction, and see Me wonderfully bring about My will. You simply relax in My wisdom and learn sensitivity to My working. Do not forget that all hearts can be moved by Me and that, with Me, the darkness will always be illuminated.

You can safely allow events to show you the way forward as long as there is My corresponding witness within your heart.

My work for you is assisted as you cultivate the person I wish you to be and as you do everything in newness of life.

Love truth.
(Zech. 8:19)

We Are Partners

Can you not sense that I am at work? I cannot overlook anything that is for your good. I am active all the time in everything that you have committed to Me; you must continue with utter trust in Me. Be conscious of My constant influence: peace giving, affecting relationships, making right.

Keep very close as we meet life's situations as partners and as you are led to what I have planned for you. You must feel our unity.

Let Me be increasingly precious to you—My Fatherhood, My understanding, My constant activity for you.

The way of love—love from you, love between us.

Turn to Me with all your heart.
(Joel 2:12)

I Shield You

My child, I allow you to see the sheer darkness within from time to time so that you may know the extent to which evil can infiltrate. But remember that your heart is toward Me. Therefore, sinful ways, repented over, are consigned to where they are powerless to affect the future.

You must always thank Me that My love has completely swallowed up the wrong and that there remains only My love.

When evil attempts to make you relive occasions of sin, when it uses circumstances to try to produce renewed guilt and fear, affirm very strongly My forgiveness as I shield you against evil's accusing voice.

There is joy in the presence of the angels of God
over one sinner who repents.
(Luke 15:10)

Let Me Lead

*H*ave you learned the lesson of resting in My love in every situation?

As my love surrounds you—assisted by your resting attitude—everything that takes place within it serves My purposes. Therefore, peace and thankfulness can prevail.

The way to victory is the rigid looking to Me, letting My strength be applied, and seeing the area of weakness or difficulty yield to My presence. Always apply My presence early.

Be content to let Me lead, which may mean the putting aside of plans, hastily formed, in which there was no clear awareness of My urging. If I am at work for you, the pace must be Mine so that harmony prevails. Do nothing out of fear as I supply your needs in My way.

————————

Learn from Me.
(Matt. 11:29)

Your Forward March

*A*lways be careful to walk in the known way—what I have revealed to you. As you firmly obey My known wishes, you can then confidently let Me lead the way in the problem areas. I know that you will keep your hand in Mine in the uncharted places and remember the power of your prayers about both people and circumstances. When a course is open for you, having sought My will, do not be hindered by misgivings. Do not try to solve every matter before taking that step with Me.

Be straightforward, seek simplicity. Nothing in your walk must be complex or in any way devious. Ensure your direction of travel, seeing all as either helping or hindering your forward march. If love is present—for Me and My children—there is no hindrance to perceiving truth.

If anyone wills to do His will, he shall know concerning
the doctrine, whether it is from God.
(John 7:17)

Let Energy Flow Outward

$\mathcal{D}$o not "feed" self in any way. Remove the motivations of self by bringing them under My victory. Immediately let the energy poured into self pour instead into concern about Me, your pleasing of Me, our communion. Let that energy flow outward in both concern and ingenuity about others' needs.

Looking away, praising, trusting in My meeting of your needs.

An iron discipline is needed, using My victory, so that you do not strive in anything motivated by self; this will ensure that the flow to others is unhindered. You will be helped by seeing Me coming between you and the pressure by evil to focus upon self and its needs. My child, as you surrender to Me, you can watch the old self-centered ways go out of your life, evil having to retreat.

He who loves his life will lose it.
(John 12:25)

Victory over Evil

Carry no burdens, except the responsibility of loving Me and serving Me. There must be no apprehension as you simply let Me lead and as you see My hand in events. Surrender to My love—ensuring your peace and influencing events—even when you are conscious of recent sinful ways.

Now more than ever, you can allow My leading—experiencing the results of My working—both in surrounding events and in My strength to respond to those events successfully. There are constant attempts by evil to destroy your peace. Do not listen to its lies. Never feel that you are at the mercy of the old ways; that is denying Me.

You have victory over evil; therefore, you must use it, walking My way of joy and courage, no matter what the circumstances.

I saw Satan fall like lightning from heaven.
(Luke 10:18)

Love Without Limit

My love resolves all conflicts, meets all needs, watches over each of your activities.

It is love without limit, a very active love on your behalf.

Continue to deliberately let all go in My love as I go before you. Make every need the subject of prayer, and instantly draw upon My strength for life's demands.

Surrender in the everyday choices is always established by My victory. Let your willingness and sacrifice produce a radical change now as you relinquish former ways.

Ask Me for an increase of love, love for those associated with you, love for all who may receive through you.

Be faithful until death, and I will give you the crown of life.
(Rev. 2:10)

Enveloped in My Love

*L*et peace reign. As you continue to rest in My love, allow that love to strengthen you to obey. Yes, enveloped in My love—this is always your immediate need.

Remember to use My presence, glorifying My name, My hands, your hands, My molding, reflecting Me.

Let there be much silence, ensuring communion with Me, with nothing false or unworthy.

As My presence and My influence increase daily, brush aside the darkness, and with resolution, walk in My light boldly.

You were precious in My sight.
(Isa. 43:4)

My Power

Evil always awaits an opportunity to bring you into sin. This *cannot* affect My promises to you as long as there are true sorrow and My forgiveness.

As you become increasingly victorious over ways of sin, you have found that occasions of falling are now vividly experienced.

When *will* you trust Me? Evil's influence is petty compared with My power.

As you surrender yourself anew to Me (at any time, no matter what has gone before), there is a changed situation.

Continue to allow My influence (steadfastly refusing doubt) as I shield you.

I have prayed for you, that your faith should not fail.
(Luke 22:32)

Choose the Light

As you deliberately choose to walk on the higher plane in the light of My presence, know that evil is powerless to influence you. In every situation it must be instinctive to choose the light.

As you keep within the brightness of My love for you, you can trust Me completely to keep evil at bay.

You know that you have a large measure of freedom—*the freedom of My love*—as long as you observe the principle of avoiding hurt to Me.

Yielding yourself to My influence every day, do not forget that a corresponding wisdom is yours, which you can follow courageously.

If you know these things, blessed are you if you do them.
(John 13:17)

Call upon Me

I want you to make My love the driving force behind each victory that you win.

Cultivate the firmness in following the way that I have shown you, without compromises. Remember the effort of choice until it becomes second nature for you.

As soon as you recognize that you are following one of the old ways, turn to the light and embrace *Me,* as you surrender the intruder.

You can call upon Me in utter trust, knowing that I will come to help you in your weakness.

Be strong . . . for I am with you.
(Hag. 2:4)

Evil's Deception

Evil frequently attempts to deceive you.

Yes, it has deceived you when it has prevented you from bringing every situation to My love; it has deceived you when forcing you to act in haste or to doubt temporarily My power to uphold and protect you; it has deceived you when leading you into fear of consequences, even though sensing that a course was My will.

Remember that although you are aware of evil's activity you need *never* be subject to it. I want you to step out, resisting all evil's challenges; you can observe Me carrying you through to victory as you defy the challenges.

Satan has asked for you, that he may sift you as wheat.
(Luke 22:31)

The Work of Transforming

My light illuminates all that is in the present, robbing it of every jarring circumstance. As My light shines *in* you, there will be unfailingly My precious peace to meet needs. Always be aware of My understanding so that you can rest upon it, letting it remove all other desire.

Bring to Me any circumstance as soon as it arises so that My immediate influence can be upon it. Do not react stressfully. Hand the matter to Me—silently where you must.

My child, I do the work of *transforming*—I make the circumstances that you give to Me work for your good because of My affection for you. Therefore, in every situation—so many not of your making—fly to Me. How can I fail you?

My burden is light.
(Matt. 11:30)

Rest Your Spirit

As you look toward the future, resolve to be true to Me, true to yourself, sensitive to the needs of those whose lives may be linked with yours.

You cannot know aspects of the days that I have in My hand for you. Here, it will be the simple following out of My way. Just lay good foundations—your walk with Me, your prayerful contacts with others.

Your future is safety in My love forever. See everything that happens on earth in relation to this truth. A partial appreciation of that ultimate experience is each day granted to you. My most solemn promise is that you will come to be with Me where I am in glory, even though by a thorny road.

Be joyful always because I will let nothing take you astray from Me.

My child, I bless you. Completely rest your spirit now in My love.

I desire that they also whom You gave Me may be with Me where I am, that they may behold My glory.
(John 17:24)

Walk the Way with Me

$\mathcal{T}$he road you have thus far walked with Me must mean the presence of more love in your heart, but deeply desire *even more*.

Let only what is of love be in you now, drawing out your love, both for Me and for My other children.

My love, reflected in you, can achieve great things; love succeeds where the intellect fails, and it succeeds where force fails. Let love dominate every aspect of your existence.

Love in its purest and truest sense will be something with which you are already partially acquainted when you finally pass into My immediate presence.

Until that time, My child, gaze into the brightness of My tender love.

Let that brightness continue to disperse fear as you walk the way with Me.

That your joy may be full.
(John 16:24)

The Way Forward

I have given you the raw material of your inheritance. In your choices and in your faithfulness to My way, I work out the enrichment of their whole being by My promises. There is a promise creation involved in that close walk with Me.

My child, when you look to Me for life's needs, that very look establishes promise fulfillment. The sense of promise in your heart becomes more sure. You see the future *filled* with Me, and you experience the gradual exclusion of all that is not of Me.

My presence shines on all your experiences and turns them into opportunities for the consolidation of your inheritance.

See My promises as far above anything that men could devise. See them as an expression of love, an eagerness for you to enjoy what I am preparing for you.

If you are tempted to feel that a promise is merely a self-created hope, immediately gaze once more into the love light of Him who watches over you. You will see that I and My promises are *indivisible*, and your trust and expectancy will return!

A state of true worship exists in that interplay of your

trust and My love. From you, I receive the assurance of your loyalty and continued walk with Me; from Me, you have the priceless sense of love shown in My promised joy and provision.

You can now see that My servants were unaffected by the conditions of life in which they were placed because of their allegiance to Me. Upholding them was the immovable hope of realizing My promises. Their fixed goal ensured their being *lifted up* into the love promise sphere, where the hurts of this world are neutralized. You, too, My child, must resolutely tread this way, letting the world's experiences merely serve to strengthen the relationship with the Promise Maker.

What you see as you look to Me is a hand outstretched, welcoming you to the realm of promise, reaching to bring you closer into that realm. This, more than all striving or planning, ensures your arrival at your true destination.

The *centrality* of My being and of the promise embodied in Me will draw together every potential of your life.

Trusting in the faithfulness of My promises means that My influence is in the foreground of your life all the time. A childlike trust in My Word represents true spiritual maturity.

My child, promises that you cherish for yourself now make the decisive difference in your spirit walk through a fallen world.

Your spirit is set free by My promises and depends for its supply not on what the world can give but on all that I am!

In Time of Need or In Life's Crises

General Themes

About the Author

John Woolley is a retired minister who has worked for many years as a hospital chaplain. He gives much of his time to pastoral work arising out of the "I Am with You" ministry, including retreats and quiet days among believers from many denominations. Woolley believes strongly in giving much time to private prayer. It was during such times that he received the "heart whispers" from God that became *I Am with You*.